Sgt Harry Tangye joined
Police at 21 years old havii
cliffs of Cornwall in Newq
years on shifts and specialis
He has attended hundreds
traffic collisions and Firearms incidents as a firearms
officer. He worked in Torquay, Plymouth and Exeter
running Sections of officers and then tripped over the
medium of Twitter soon raising 10's of thousands of
followers and becoming an influential voice in policing
not only in his own Force but nationally too. He was
the overall winner for the Police Twitter Awards 2016
and retired from service in 2020.

Firearms and Fatals

An Autobiography of 30 Years Frontline Policing Exposed

Sgt Harry Tangye

The views and opinions expressed in this book are those of the author and the contributors alone and do not necessarily represent those of Her Majesty's Government or the Home Office or any other Government agency. The author has endeavoured to report events accurately and truthfully and any insult or injury to any of the parties described, named or quoted herein is unintentional.

Every effort has been made to obtain the necessary permissions with reference to copyright material, both illustrative and quoted. The publishers will be happy to correct any inaccuracies in later editions.

To my wife Rebecca who has been the most incredible unwavering support from the start, apart from Twitter, she never understood Twitter! And to my two children Rowan and Savannah.

ACKNOWLEDGEMENTS

First and foremost, I would like to thank my parents Moira and Nigel Tangye who brought me up to appreciate life, not money and to never fear doing what I aspired to do.

I want to thank my wonderful wife Rebecca, or Becky to me and I am the only one permitted to call her that! She was there as a 19 year old bride when I was in my probation and supported the stresses, the tears and the joys of a 30 year policing career. My life would have been very different and not nearly so enriched without her. Thank you to my wonderful two children, now 20 year olds who have been next to no trouble at all and have given their parents the simplest of jobs in bringing them up. They will both be truly amazing people in life.

I would like to bring special notice to my friend of 25 years Sgt Olly Tayler QPM who has also been there with support and beers whenever they were required. A similar friendship is one everyone should have to get them through life.

Thank you to my Chief Constable Shaun Sawyer who has been an unbelievable example to me on how to be courageous, stick up for your beliefs and above all, value people. My Twitter page would have been closed in week two if it hadn't been for him.

My Deputy Chief Constable Paul Netherton OBE has been just as influential. He's been a hugely strong and courageous figure who has stuck his neck out from time to time to speak out on things which weren't right. He has supported me throughout and I personally thank him for his kindness and backing.

I'd like to thank Mike Pannett who has been the most incredible support in my latter policing career and his guidance through my Twitter years. A mate who's always at the end of the phone and who's energy I only wish I could muster.

Dave Wardell has changed laws with Finns Law, and a blog within this book *'Break a window or stab a police dog, the law says it's the same'* was written with him in mind. He is a truly remarkable man who has given me enormous strength and friendship. His book *Fabulous Finn published by Quercus* shows what a character of a man he is and it has been an honour to know him.

Thank you to someone who I can call a friend Nick Knowles who has given much advice and support and whose friendship I value and John Nichol who not only wrote *Spitfire published by Simon & Schuster* putting much content on my father in it, but has since become a friend too, although he may not agree!

Thank you to my dear friend Colin Taylor the author of *The Life of a Scilly Sergeant published by Century* who has given me advice and influenced the beginning of this book.

Not exactly to do with the book, but I would like to thank my dear friend Chris Beer for arranging a Spitfire flight for me, a flight that brought me closer to

8

my late father Nigel Tangye who had been an air reconnaissance Spitfire pilot in the Second World War. Chris allowed me to understand how my father felt in the plane whilst he was avoiding the enemy, a truly unique experience.

Thank you also to Jeff Gillard who has accompanied me on many a shift and has helped keep my head relatively sane with our chats and Cornish breaks with our mad and wonderful friends!

Thank you from the bottom of my heart to Alex Mattingly who was press ganged by his wonderful wife Jo, into correcting most of the mistakes in this book. I'm truly grateful to them both!

Thank you to Arthur, my Border Jack Russell Cross.

9

CONTENTS

Acknowledgements

Prologue   Pg 12

1. Breaching the Terrorism Act   Pg 15
2. In the Beginning   Pg 18
3. Life on Patrol   Pg 31
4. What a Set-up!   Pg 42
5. The Beautiful Couple   Pg 46
6. Car and Foot Pursuits   Pg 52
7. Helicopters and Machete's   Pg 64
8. Looking in The Eyes of Dead People   Pg 71
9. A Road Collision   Pg 74
10. Taking the Fight to them   Pg 84
11. Night Time Economy   Pg 95
12. Wives, Dogs and Children!   Pg 109
13. The Dark   Pg 118
14. Childbirth and Promotion   Pg 127
15. A Debt Repaid   Pg 144
16. @DC_ARVSgt – Twitter   Pg 155
17. What Lengths to Save a Man's Life?   Pg 176
18. How Hard Can it be to Shoot Right?   Pg 181
19. Never Sit in the Comfortable Seat   Pg 189
20. Bravery   Pg 193
21. The Gravel Driveway   Pg 202
22. VIP Protection   Pg 208
23. Ingredients to Make a Police Officer   Pg 219
24. This is What 140mph Looks Like!   Pg 232
25. Snitches get Stitches   Pg 238
26. Selfie on the Bridge   Pg 242
27. How to Stay Alive as a Police Officer   Pg 250

BLOGS

28. Break a Window or Stab a Police Dog,
    The Law Says it's the Same. Well it did!   Pg 256
29. A Quite Unusual Routine   Pg 262
30. Taser - A Tool for the Pacifists   Pg 268
31. The Knot is Getting Tighter   Pg 276
32. Car Collision   Pg 282
33. We Need You but We don't Want You   Pg 286
34. Spit Hoods/Guards. To Use or Not to Use?   Pg 292
35. A Diversion from my Everyday Life   Pg 297

Prologue

I'm sprinting across Lusty Glaze Road in Newquay in Cornwall after my quarry. He's darting from left to right, then disappears down a bank towards the sheer drop of the cliff. I'm not put off and determined to carry on but it's getting tricky. I slip down on my backside, down the steep mounds of sea pinks which frame the top of the cliffs and hope I can halt my slide in time. I slide a good 2 metres and my foot gains purchase to a ridge leaving little time to spare. My quarry is skilfully skipping along the narrow ledge and around a rock jutting out of the cliff face, I follow and lose my balance slightly, my shoulders desperately reaching back towards the cliffside but having a deadly attraction towards the edge as well. I see the rocks some 30 metres below with the turbulent Cornish sea crashing against them, and I have a bolt of adrenaline rush through me. I collapse my knees which saves me from a certain fatal fall. I look at the path, shrug myself off and continue my futile chase but with slightly less enthusiasm. By the time I reach the rock and gain the view from the other side, I see nothing but a vertical bank and a small rabbit hole. I was 10 years old, and this was my playground.

20 Years later, and I've slewed my BMW patrol car to a halt and I'm running after my quarry in much the same way but I have a Glock 17 pistol in my right hand, and I'm being weighed down with body armour and heavy boots, a Taser, a Baton and handcuffs, and instead of the towering cliffs and sea pinks, I'm running through the streets of Exeter. Instead of a rabbit, it's a 6 ft tall

man with a hoodie dragged over his head to cover his identity. He's sprinting away having waved a gun at some unsuspecting and now petrified teenager outside of a local pub. He's clearly determined to get away and I am just as determined he's not going to.

How I got from one foot chase along those cliffs to chasing this man with a gun is a tale of many adventures, and now I'm at the end of a 30 year career in policing, 24 of those years carrying a gun and driving fast cars I think it's time to tell a few of those stories.

I do have a wry chuckle at the current Lusty Glaze beach where I was brought up some 50 metres from it. I sit there sometimes on the golden sands with my Terrier dog Arthur and look up at those same cliffs where I so very nearly fell to my death. It meant so little to me then, schools never banged on about health and safety so we took our chances when we could. I gaze at the adventure activities this wonderful beach now offers including rock climbing, abseiling and zip wires. I could see the carefully engineered securing points with ropes dangling past those same sea pinks with fit young people straddling the rope gingerly moving their torso towards the bottom, foot by foot, adjusting their safety helmets as they regain their composure. How, as that 10-year old, I would have dashed passed them chuckling as I did so, constantly looking out for further adventure.

1. Breaching the Terrorism Act

Poacher turned gamekeeper they say, and even though I wasn't a thief or a burglar I was into explosives in quite a big way when I was 12 years old. Things start from small beginnings but it soon became apparent with my newly formed Crime Busters gang, formed with my close friends Nicholas and Richard, that if you started with weed killer and mixed sugar with it, it made a lot of smoke when lit, and we soon developed it by pouring it into empty glass Corona bottles.

I think it was my bright idea to not only drop a match in and see it explode into a thousand tiny shards of glass, but if I was to quickly screw the top on afterwards, surely this would create more pressure and better results. The next thing I realise is there is an awful lot of blood running down my leg and face and I am cycling my custom-built regency green bicycle with cow horn handlebars as fast as my dwindling blood-filled body would take me to Newquay casualty unit. Having arrived exhausted and rather dizzy from loss of blood, my story becoming more embellished every time I tell it, the nurses having surveyed my blood sodden jumper and trousers thought a car crash victim had just stumbled in and I suspect never quite believed my 'falling off my bike' explanation. One piece of glass had severed some rather busy blood motorways in my leg so this was probably my second near brush with death... but I was undeterred, and I had to improve the design of my cottage industry incendiary device that I suspect would have given me a good 20-year sentence or more under the terrorism act today.

The Crime Busters gang was developing nicely even though there was little crime busting occurring and probably more crimes being committed if I'm entirely honest but this wasn't a concern in my Cornish 12 year old mind. We compacted scaffolding poles full of our deadly concoction having crimped one end and then rammed a broom handle into the other. I drilled a hole through the thick metal in the centre and then covered it in sellotape to stop leakage of the substance. It was now portable.

We cycled across to Pentire beach just south of Newquay where we believed it would be completely isolated and safe to carry out our test. The day of the testing was nigh, and we placed the prototype out onto the sand at the foot of the cliff. I looked around the vast empty beach, the blue sky and the sea lazily dropping in at low tide some 100 metres away. This was the time and the place. I looked at Richard, his podgy face with freckles holding the matches in his shaking hand. Nick was standing wisely behind a large rock murmuring, "I'm not sure we should be doing this". But it was time and I took the matches from Richard and approached the Crime Buster Bomb.

There was no going back and I lit the match. It snapped off and fell into the sand. I took another out of the box and struck it slightly more gently and it flared into life, then calmed to a candle flame. I held it to the sellotape covered hole and touched it. A second later and the carefully drilled hole in the pipe is erupting with spitting fire and smoke and I'm turning on my heels for the same rock that Nick was hiding behind.

"Rich, Rich, get back here!" I shout as I see he is transfixed to the spot with an incredulous grin on his face staring at the spitting bomb. He then shakes himself out of his trance and runs behind the rock to the relative safety of what I now realise is a small rock not big enough for three 12-year olds to hide behind safely.

Now to say the explosion was loud is a total understatement. I mean this was loud, really very loud. We stood up from behind the rock, noticing immediately the pipe had gone from its original position and in its place was a large dustbin lid sized divot. There was shrapnel still landing around us in postage-stamp sized shards of thick scaffolding metal and the boom of a thousand shotguns was still echoing around the cliffs. The boom was replaced by the rising of a thousand seagulls screeching loudly raised from their lazy slumber by this new yob culture that had just disturbed them and as we looked at each other... we heard Police sirens.

We ran up the cliffs to the getaway pedal bikes and shot down the path towards civilisation, our theory being we could blend in to the built up area but were sticking out like beacons on the cliffs where we were and from where the acrid yellow smoke had not yet cleared. We managed to escape and I didn't hear anything more about it. I suspect the sirens were a complete coincidence but my explosives factory days were over. We were done, and I think it probably saved our lives by ending it... again.

2.   In the Beginning

I lived a wonderful existence in my childhood; I seem to be one of the lucky few who had an idyllic upbringing in a beautiful place. We never had money, but I had the biggest playground around me to run around in, the Cornish cliffs, the beaches and the fields.

I managed to get the interest of a feared member of my secondary school called Mike. He owned several Lurcher dogs, one of whom was called Kim. A beautiful gentle dog until she caught the sight of a rabbit when she turned into a deadly missile running at 35mph until she knocked the startled rabbit off its feet. Having a 'hard man' as a friend was particularly useful but I knew I had to be careful to stay out of trouble or at least not get caught but I was more than happy to wake up to his tapping my bedroom window and me climb out to join him for some lamping. This was a system of catching rabbits by using a motorbike battery and headlight whereby the rabbits were highlighted and dazzled for the incoming Kim. It's something I couldn't possibly do today as my love for animals is far too strong but not quite enough to reach to vegetarianism so popular today, and it now happens to be illegal but at 3am on a school night it was what we did for a couple of hours.

Mike was adept at the killing side of things, very slick with the karate action at the back of the neck despatching the rabbit instantly. He would always take the rabbits home with him for Kim and him to enjoy later. I felt it a little suspicious for me to tell Mum and Dad I had suddenly found some rabbit meat we could use. Always wanting to take things one bit further, I decided to make a pencil case for school out of one of the rabbit skins. Google not being available and really not being too bothered to go to the library I decided that recalling something about using salt was all I needed to know.

I went to work preparing the pelt rubbing some salt into the skin until I was quite happy and after just 5 minutes the job was done. I used a needle and thread to bring the two sides together and was quite proud of the job I'd done. The fur is a beautiful soft quality and I knew my friends at school may be not only just a little surprised, but quite impressed at my hunting prowess. Mike thought I was nuts of course and decided he was going to have no part of it.

I think it was about 3 weeks later that I was still trying to convince not only my friends but also myself that my newly acquired rabbit pencil case was not in fact a pungent rotting carcass that needed to be abandoned with all its contents. My early attempts at recycling and saving the world were to be put off for another few years, or until David Attenborough could persuade me he was better at it than I was.

My rabbit catching continued into using Mike's ferrets, again when we were in our early teens. They stink to high heaven which immediately put me off from owning any but he was very fond of them. We ended up climbing down a slippery narrow ledge half way down a cliff. Again, utter madness but we had spotted a rabbit hole down there and we were determined to get to it. Mike went first with the ferret in his hand and I closely

19

followed him, trying to convince both him and me I wasn't completely terrified. One glance down at the rocks far below was enough to confirm to myself this was a terrible idea, but I'm sure we would be all right.

It was a beautiful sunny day, I'd say the rocks were a good 30 metres below, the tide was out, and as we were now standing above a large cave below us, there was nowhere to slide down if we did lose our footing. The ledge meant I would hold on to the grass tufts of sea pinks with my right hand and walk like a ballerina with one foot in front of the other using my left arm to balance. Once we had got to the rabbit hole I could see Mike pondering somewhat as the hole was slightly obscured by an outcrop just above it. He popped the ferret down the hole but then grabbed the tuft firmly with both hands giving it a yank. The tuft came away much more easily than he expected erupting in an explosion of earth, sea pinks and grass which fell like confetti around us, and Mike was waving both his arms like windmills imitating the best impression of slow motion falling I have ever seen.

He rotated on his left foot so his body swung to face his destiny that had once been behind him, and all he could do was slump down to his buttocks in order to hopefully find some form of purchase on the grass ledge. I was momentarily stunned into seeing my friend begin his fall to certain death not a foot in front of me when my reflexes cut in and I made a stab at the back of his jacket with my left hand, holding on for dear life to the grass with my right. I got quite a good hold of his collar but it forced me down to my knees before I could stop his fall. We both paused in utter fear feeling the surging adrenaline rushing around our bodies and on realising all was not over, started the oh so gentle operation of hauling him back up over the ledge to recover panting and exhausted on the rabbit footpath we had settled on. There was a scuffle above us and a light cream ferret popped his head out of the hole without any rabbit and with an expression of utter confusion on its face if ever you could get that on a ferret but I swear it did!

It was as we made our way back from our empty rabbit hole and a near cliff fall that I realised Mike's head was pouring with blood. A lump of the tuft was in fact a small rock but had made a good effort of cutting into his scalp. We suspected the rabbits had planted this device to stop any selfish humans entering their domain and it had worked. Either they had been out at the time but more than likely they had moved out to a more suitable home. Now what to do with Mike's bleeding head gushing with crimson blood by now and with no parents at home I managed to come up with some ridiculous excuse to a neighbour who kindly took us to hospital. I guess that was yet another time I nearly died. I was finding that playing outside could be quite dangerous yet each experience was teaching me the world had clearly more chances in it than I first perceived.

Because of all this water, it was natural for me to take up swimming and gain lifesaving qualifications I had led an even more exotic life of lifeguarding Lusty Glaze Beach in Newquay, the most wonderful time of baking in the sun and cooling off in the icy sea and maybe hiring the odd deckchair out as well to earn some of my wage. I realised I needed to show any potential police employer i.e. the Devon and Cornwall Police, I could hold my own and I was able to prove myself to be an extremely mature member of the British public and not the immature just out of school teenager I actually was. Having gained a handful of mediocre O'levels including a CSE grade 3 in French I was particularly proud of, I became a community service volunteer in London looking after the mentally and physically disabled. No apologies to anyone who may be upset with my term, I have no idea if it is correct, wrong, damned right insulting but at the time it was fine and didn't upset anyone. My first day was not without incident.

I drove in my Triumph Dolomite car I'd bought in an auction in Falmouth for just £130 to London and was more surprised than anyone to almost get there but it promptly broke down on a major roundabout on the North Circular and therefore having arranged the AA to pick it up found my way to Kitchener House in Hornsey which was to be my home for the next year. This Victorian house was a half-way house for the disabled where they were living as much of an independent life as possible but were also having intrusive assistance by staff and volunteers who would circulate within all their flats helping them with everyday chores. The house was made up of a series of flats on each floor designated for each resident. I was to live in a room on the top floor and I loved every moment. I shared my room with a Turkish guy called Ishak Aci - completely wrong spelling but my English is terrible and my Turkish is even worse. He was like a big brother to me and introduced me to my first kebab! I remember his astonishment when he learned I had never shared the delights of a kebab before and was determined to get that put right immediately. On arrival at the house however, I was greeted with instructions on how to make tea for the staff ensuring I held the OCD manager's mug by the handle and not the rim. Being expected to make the tea is no doubt grounds for bullying accusations today but do you know, I didn't feel it in any way and I felt I had been accepted even if only at ground level for now. I was then asked how I felt about cleaning residents who had... quite frankly, shat themselves. I think he was a little surprised when I replied, "Well, we'll just have to see won't we?"

On feeling rather homesick and completely out of my comfort zone, I made my way to my room and realised I had lost my wallet with all my worldly goods in cash, feeling quite devastated for a whole week until I was told by the wonderful garage owner they had fixed my car for next to nothing and they had found my wallet under the car mat. I couldn't believe it either. London must be a city of honest people, I thought!

With regards to the wiping of pooh from the bottoms of adults, I realised I wasn't that bothered to be honest and have had my hands in far worse since. I can detach myself from it psychologically and with a high pressure hose physically and I have found what's helped is that I've always had empathy for the person who through no fault of their own provided such a contribution. In this case it would be because the young man in his 20s had released his bowels probably without even knowing at first, and then delaying telling me for as long as possible so it would be 5 minutes prior to the end of my shift that the tell-tale signs would flood the nostrils of all those around and I would take him to their bathroom to clean him up. Often confined to a wheelchair, you could feel their embarrassment and even at my age of 18 then, I felt for them. I wondered how I would have felt if I had been in their position and I knew I was the luckiest man alive to be able to help and not to have to rely on that help. This experience has stayed with me all my life.

12 months later and I'm applying for the Devon and Cornwall Police. I had my Gold Duke of Edinburgh Award, easily worth a couple of A levels I would say and I had had a good year working in Kitchener House, which had been a huge education including the time when another resident worker walked into my room saying, "Harry, I think I've been stabbed" whilst holding his bright red blood-stained white T shirt together around his gaping stomach wound.

Well at this point of my tale of a privileged upbringing and no abusive parents, I can add that I had also completed 2 weeks of puking on the Tall Ships Sailing scheme and I had jumped out of an aircraft for a sponsored lifesaving event to prove I was the perfect recruit for the police. It was only when the aircraft was spluttering up the runway for take-off like a battered petrol mower that I suddenly realised I had never been on a plane before. It was some 2 years later having only taken off in a plane for my parachute jump that I eventually landed in one when I flew away on a holiday.

Armed with all this worldly experience of puking on tall ships and throwing myself out of planes, I applied for the Police and got through to the interview stage. Three days of assessments at Police Headquarters and I'm sitting outside the interview room waiting to be called in for the result. I was called back in and sat before the panel of three waiting for my acceptance. I think after the 3 minute constructive criticism speech they were basically telling me to 'Grow up!' I mean, a mature man like me at 19 years old! It was suggested I needed to get some worldly experience and perhaps join the Special Constables. I was devastated. More devastated that anyone has ever been in their life, or so I thought but when my grieving period had subsided I applied for the Specials and had the most wonderful time in Newquay and then Launceston for a couple more years.

I couldn't let this time go without saying what wearing the uniform for the first time was like. Special Constables are given far more official training now, and have to do a lot of pre-loaded work before even going out on the street. They are volunteers but have all the powers of a full time police officer which is pretty cool, and you do get expenses. No duck house expenses can be claimed though, just mileage. In my day it was a matter of being given your uniform and attending a weekly get-together where they would discuss law, and very much encouraged skills such as stop search.

I remember walking out of Newquay police station to assist with the Carnival on my very first assignment. I was to stand on a point opposite the station. I was dressed in black trousers, a wooden truncheon hanging down my inside trouser leg in the specific truncheon pocket which I thought was pretty sneaky, a white shirt, black tie and blue NATO jumper. Oh my God, I felt like a king, until I stepped into the public domain and hoped to God no one would ask me a question. I felt the whole world was looking at me wondering why the hell some kid was wearing that police uniform. I would listen to my police radio and be scared to death I was asked to reply on it. It was quite a feeling. I stood on my point feeling like a fraud. I mean really, how can I be permitted to wear this uniform? A little later on I would crew up with regular officers and knew that this was the job for me. It was the realisation that I was in a gang that had back up, that it was out to do good, to look after and support those that needed us, and to drag bullies into justice often kicking and screaming. They were no longer the ones doing the bullying, terrorising their wives, beating them within an inch of their lives. I knew that no matter what, as long as I was determined, I could right any wrong. I was finally in the proper Crime Buster's I'd always wanted. My Crime Buster's gang was finally preventing and detecting crime, not producing it, I had made it. Well, nearly. I needed to get into the regulars like I wanted nothing else.

I made a great group of friends and avoided those that didn't like Specials. As I say, I think the relationship has got a lot better now but Special Constables were relatively new then and some officers felt they were overtime takers because they were putting a Special Constable at a location or doubling up a regular with one instead of paying overtime for other regulars to do the same. I would join a regular section for a late shift which was nothing but fun in Newquay in the summer, all those fights outside Sailors Pub but loving diving into every one of them. We would nick them, cuff them and bundle them into vans. Next to no paperwork, no risk assessments, little statistic collecting for the government which no one believes anyway, literally hours of extra time for real policing instead.

I think becoming a Special Constable was just the best thing that could have happened to me then. I often say to young officers that it's not what happens, it's how you deal with it. I could have sulked off and gone in a different direction licking my wounds to do something else instead, but I had taken their advice and joined the Specials. I soon realised I had to think on my feet. On attending a domestic dispute with a regular officer, I remember the male in the house shouting at me,

"What the hell does he know about anything, that spotty git is just out of school".

My colleague looked at me smiling with an 'over to you' expression. I surprised myself with a total lie. Yes, I lied with absolutely no shame. I replied, "I may look young and thanks for that, but I'm 25 and have 2 children. I understand the issues here as I myself am going through a divorce".

There was stunned silence by all including my colleague. The male froze his expression of disbelief which relaxed slightly; he looked me up and down and then said, "Right, right, well you will know what a pain in the ass women can be then". My colleague took over for me whilst I was ahead.

I so very much enjoyed my time as a Special Constable and took every opportunity I could to work with a shift attending road accidents, domestics and street fights. There was becoming a point however that I had to get a half decent job just in case I failed to get into the police at all and Newquay being a seasonal town was not able to supply me with that. It was a very nervous time. I had had a taste of what I wanted to do long term and as a Special I was fearless and often tackled people a lot bigger than myself because I knew there were other good people there to back me up. I wanted to be a part of this team permanently and doing anything else just wasn't going to cut it. It did help my drive to join all the more when at the age of 19, I was in one particular struggle with a male who had assaulted two others and was putting up quite a fight and whilst my colleague and I were bundling him into the back of the police van, I heard a young girl's voice shout excitedly "Wow, it's Harry from school, that is so cool". She was the most beautiful girl I knew then, way out of my league but she was a girl I had fancied the pants off quite frankly but I had had little chance of achieving my fantasy! We shall move on; shall we? Her long dark flowing hair wrapped around her slim face with that beaming smile of pearly white teeth. I was transfixed. Here was someone way out of my league I thought, and suddenly I felt I had moved from Halifax division 4, to second from the bottom of division 3. Let's not get too hasty now. She walked away into the night and my fantasy was over.

Back down to division 4 but it had felt good for that moment.

Fast forward to the job at Launceston leisure centre. From lifeguard to shift supervisor it made me all the more determined to join the police full-time. Don't get me wrong, I enjoyed the people but Christ it was dull. Sitting in a steamy swimming pool watching women of a certain age swim breaststroke up and down chatting to each other with the longest necks they could contort to keep their perms dry. This was not the life for me.

So I applied for the police again when I was 21 years old and made it through the application process to the 3-day interview again. I felt better for it this time because I had already been through the process once and knew what to expect. First things first, the medical. Blood pressure taken and the Doctor said, 'Hmm, a bit high, I suggest you go away and lie down and relax for half an hour and come back."

"RELAX?" I'm lying on my bed willing my heart to stop hitting the ceiling. It was pounding so hard shouting at me, nay screaming and laughing at my police career going down the swanny before it had even started. I was going to have to go back to that blessed swimming pool. Oh Christ, maybe if I held my breath, no it goes faster, okay I'm doomed. Maybe think of a peaceful tide rolling onto the beach and I'm lying in the sun. That's better... calmly does it, yes, that's better, now check my pulse. "JESUS, 120!!"

I go back to the police Doctor and sit in front of him. I can feel the adrenaline surging through my veins. I'm a defeated soul. I despondently say, "It's no good, Doctor, I can feel my heart coming out of my chest."

He pumps the pressure pump, looks at the vertical glass tube and stares at me in silence. Then he turns away and says very matter of factly, "Oh, that's much better".

He was lying out of his pants, and I loved him for it.

And so three days later I am sitting there again, sitting in the corridor outside the same room I had been turned down from the Devon and Cornwall Police 2 years earlier. I was scared, very scared. The other applicants were excited for making it so far, but I realised I had been there before and had had the crushing news of failure. I was called back into the room and listened intently to the first 6 words and none of the rest. "We are pleased to tell you.... "

I just bet you just checked there were six words then didn't you?

I had the biggest grin on my face you can imagine. I just couldn't believe my luck. I was in the Police... bloody hell, I'd only just gone and done it!

The training college was a place called Chantmarle in Dorset. A manor house, far too gorgeous to train young recruits in but I got through that and passed out in 1990. My first station was to be Torquay. Things just couldn't be better!

3. Life on patrol

I spent the most wonderful 2 years in Torquay during my probation. I felt a complete fake and out of my depth for the first few months but gradually got my confidence and having been cleared for independent patrol I attended the briefing for the expected fanfare and celebration of my success into independence. To my disappointment, there was none but instead the anti-climax of having a set of panda car keys pushed across the table towards me by the Sergeant. I was still staggered however. I was going to drive my own police car, on my own, with no one else, I mean really, no one else? Were they completely mad?! I couldn't wait to get a call, my first call. I drove out of the police station and was convinced I was going to crash the car immediately with all eyes on me. I felt everyone was looking at me, judging me. They'd all point and laugh soon, wouldn't they? To be completely honest with you I cannot remember my first job. Probably because I had been a Special Constable for some time but this was different. It sounds strange still, but I have never been one to remember important dates or occasions. I have no idea why. I don't remember the date I joined the police, my first arrest, I don't remember the date my father died when I was still a teenager, I don't visit his grave as in my mind, he's not there. I don't do all those special occasion things, those things that others feel are so important to them. I look at anniversaries of death as meaningless. I used to feel quite bad about this but I realised to me life was a date of when someone was born and the day they died, and there were some seasons between. When they are dead, they are dead, and I prefer to remember them every day and smile at the good memories, not have it in my mental diary to remember them one day a year.

Having diverted from the subject somewhat, I now get back to my first day on patrol. There was no adult next to me or expecting me to hand things on for them to check. Being a Special hadn't taught me these skills as they were less involved in the paperwork then. We had all the fun without all the paperwork. I do remember in my early days of the regulars when I did attend incidents, the caller or informant I spoke to did assume I knew how to do my job when although having gone through the training, I really felt quite out of my depth. The best advice I had from my tutors was as long as I had someone's name and address I could always recover a situation later. This has saved my bacon several times since.

I was regularly reminded of my naivety. I was searching someone's flat for drugs and they were in the lounge with me and my tutor constable when I came across a large box of syringes still in their plastic packaging. I looked at the label on the side of them which stated the intended use for them being for insulin, and without thinking said, "Oh, who has diabetes here?"

This may not have been completely embarrassing if the suspect hadn't said, "Oh bless him, is he new?"

How I so wished the ground had swallowed me up with my naivety in tow. These simple events reminded me of how so very inexperienced and still so very naïve I was.

Time went on and I was gaining more confidence; I worked in Dawlish for 3 years which taught me to work in isolated areas where back-up was not very forthcoming. I was with a crewmate and we were called to a pub where a well-known yob had been causing trouble and was refusing to leave. My colleague Faye looked through the pub window and suggested we wait for backup from Teignmouth, a Police Station some 5 miles away. Maybe it was my arrogance, or even my ego, but having glanced at the relatively peaceful pub, I said, "No, we should be okay".

It was approximately 4 minutes later when I was smashing through the pub swing doors with the youth grabbed by his shirt with my two hands and I was falling on top of him. I had asked him to leave the pub and he had replied, "Come and throw me out then, if you've got the f'ing bottle".

The decision had been relatively easy. Well extremely easy in fact because if I hadn't got the bottle, I wouldn't have been able to Police in Dawlish again, and anyway it may be a little fun. Having received a soft landing by collapsing on the youth, things went a little quiet for a couple of seconds. I saw Faye standing above me and I thought, "Well that went rather well". It was only then the pub doors flew open again and the friends of my drain on society still tightly in my grasp, flew out of the pub with the main aim of freeing their freshly arrested colleague. My ego and their loyalty to their friend fought on for several minutes with Faye somewhere in the middle. My radio went flying, my clip on tie disappeared, my jumper ripped and my cap was never to be seen again. I had to see my prisoner dissolve within the angry crowd with me looking a little worse for wear unable to retrieve him. Fortunately for my conscience Faye was just fine but I did feel terrible for putting her into such unnecessary danger. As they wandered off I shouted, "Gents, there'll be a knock in the morning", and indeed there was, with a big red metal key at approximately 6.30am and the message was received. Don't think you can do that to her Majesty's Police Officers and get away with it. We will win.

We'll stay in Dawlish with my next little tale. One mixed with belly-laughing and sadness. I had been pursuing an Audi A80 around Dawlish in the evening for some time and it had headed for the hills. You very soon realise whether or not you are going to be able to stay with the car or not. A pursuit settles down to a rhythm really, and it's only a matter of time before it ends, either because they fall off a bend or because you have run him towards a stinger device with one of your colleagues dragging it out in front of him.

I suspected he may be a drink-driver and as it was very rural I was happy to allow this to carry on the way it was. The driver was going at a fair old rate, and my marked police Escort was doing well to keep up with it. It suddenly turned off up a farm track at such a pace it was bouncing over the ruts and seemed all over the place. The instant decision by myself to do the same meant I had considerably blurred vision for a short time, wondering if my little Escort would make the next

50 metres or so of rough terrain and I soon realised I was losing traction as my tyres were spinning and I was not getting any closer to the Audi in front. I wasn't getting any further away from it either however, seeing the Audi was also wheel spinning and we had that comic moment when we both had pedal to the metal and yet neither of us were making any progress up the hill whatsoever.

The simple task of getting out of my car without slipping over in the mud, walking up to the bemused Audi driver still spinning his tyres and tapping on the window to make the arrest, took all of a couple of minutes. Having taken him back to the station in my car, I returned with the Sgt to recover the Audi from this farm track. Sgt Ian Warne was a portly chap with a wonderful smile and an infectious laugh, more of a chuckle really and a pleasure to be around. The Audi was stuck in the mud and so I advised Sgt Warne that he stand to the side of the passenger door so he didn't get covered in mud from the rear tyres when I span them to free the car.

With the Sgt safely out of the way I attempted to release the Audi from the mud by rolling it down the hill with a gentle application of accelerator but it wasn't going anywhere so I gave it full power to see what would happen. Still nothing so I turned the steering wheel to the full right lock to gain some purchase maintaining the drive but again nothing. I released the accelerator wondering what to try next when I heard a gentle knock on the passenger door window. I got out of the car and went around to speak to Sgt Warne. The vision before me convinced me the Audi A8 was indeed front wheel drive and turning the steering fully to the right had put the fully ejected mud scooped up by the front tyres straight up and over poor Sgt Warne. He stood there like a Laurel and Hardy sketch, motionless like a sculpture in chocolate beginning to melt. I was horrified wondering what his reaction would be only to be completely relieved when he slowly raised both hands up to his circular John Lennon glasses removing them from his face in comic timing to reveal two perfectly flesh pink circles around his eyes. The silence was broken by his body shaking as he broke out into his familiar chuckle and we both collapsed in laughter. "Tangye!" He shouted, "What have you done to me?"

Sgt Warne died of natural causes far too early in life. I miss that man.

I then worked 3 wonderful years in Paignton on the incident car. A time in my life which contained numerous stories, some I couldn't repeat here but some I will dare tell you having now retired at the time of publication!

I met someone here in Paignton who later became my best friend for many years. He is Sgt 4338 Olly Tayler and we have been each other's wingmen together for the past 25 years. We have so much on each other if one was to press the button and let our secrets out we would both implode! Knowledge is security and I recommend everyone have one Olly. Everyone needs someone they can go to, to complain about work or home life when it gets you down, or when you fail a course or you have had bad news, it's a necessary requirement of policing and probably any other career I suggest. We have flown Merlin Helicopters together, thanks to his wonderful brother James Tayler who went and spoilt everything by emigrating to New Zealand where he's currently a Rescue Helicopter Pilot. We've been winched down on lifeboats from RAF Sea Kings, and we've been to many a Culdrose Pilots' BBQ. It's been a riot to be truthful.

I was introducing Olly to Torbay when he joined us from his probation station of Plymouth so I was showing him the ropes on a busy Saturday foot patrol through the main street of Paignton. There was a long queue of stationary traffic caused by the level crossing being closed for an approaching train, but unfortunately one motorist had not been concentrating quite so much as others and had become marooned on a pedestrian crossing enabling no right of passage for unfortunate shoppers, and members of Her Majesty's Constabulary. The driver glanced at me in terror. He was bang to rights and he furtively glanced across to his scowling "I told you so" wife next to him. I stood next to the car for a second. Olly was looking at me, and there were a number of the public wondering what I was going to do. Some scowls willing me to slam my truncheon on its roof, and many others probably thinking, "Give the guy a break, we've all done it", so I decided there was only one thing for it. I opened the rear passenger door and to Olly's surprise, and certainly the occupants of the car, I got into the back of the car and whilst sliding my backside across to the other side of the car said, "Morning!" before opening the other passenger door and getting out on the other side. Point made and everyone was happy. Fortunately, the traffic started moving before any other pedestrians decided to follow.

On a similar foot patrol, I came across a young miscreant named Steven. He was a known burglar, 18 years old but looked 12 so his cover to being found by a resident in their house was to say he was looking for his cat and he would always get away with it. There he was and I had him cornered. Knowing he was up to no good, mainly because he was living and breathing, I informed him I was going to carry out a stop search on him. He had a huge previous history of burglaries and showed no sign yet of listening to the advice he was offered by many a professional. You have to consider his full-time job was preying off vulnerable elderly victims and as he treated them as objects, his conscience was completely clear.

I can see the PC brigade having kittens over this poor boy being picked on and stereotyped but if those same people had listened a bit more to us cops instead of those that criticised "Stop Search" so much then we perhaps wouldn't have the horrific situation where criminals feel they have free reign to carry all their weapons, drugs and ill-gotten gains around our public streets as they do, and oh a lot fewer deaths from stabbings would have occurred I have absolutely no doubt.

I feel they are very much responsible but they either seem to have disappeared or like Mayor of London Sadiq Khan, simply changed their minds having been part of the cause of so much devastation in their wake simply from not listening or trusting those who knew the job. Because taxpayers pay for the Police, many feel that entitles them to tell the police what works best. It doesn't, it shouldn't but unfortunately the Police Force became a service and we had to listen to the community however ridiculous some of their views were. Absolutely fine in practice but unfortunately in reality meant the politicians and many senior police leaders listened to the ones that shouted the loudest and not to the ones who had something to say. Extremists and those with huge anti police agendas had a field day, taking advantage of gullible leaders and those who were paralysed by political correctness. Politics interfered with policing more than it ever did before and we had to change with the wind whichever way it blew, crazy and frustrating if you were on the end of this.

Anyway, coming back to my tale of persecuting this poor chap who had had the bad luck of being caught many times in the past causing much misery to other law-abiding citizens, I carried out a search only to find in the lid of a Lypsyl tube, a tiny bit of cannabis. I looked at him and he looked at me. We weren't talking crime of the century here, were we? So I already knew what would be the best course of action. Today I would have given him a caution for it on the spot and placed it in the drugs register for destruction but to be honest, my exhibits bag would have resembled very much like an empty one!

It was very different then, but the intention was very much the same. I needed to do something that told him he couldn't think he could carry illegal drugs around the streets in front of cops however insignificant the amount may be and was proportionate for that level of offence but maybe I could have a little fun at the same time. For the PC brigade, this is where you can type up your claims of human rights breaches; however you can save your laptop battery because this was pre-Human Rights Act when we were able to have some fun and yet no harm was done either.

I therefore took a coin out of my pocket and said, "Well Steven, heads or tails?"

He was rather bemused and asked me for some clarification on the matter but not in such eloquent language so I explained that I wanted him to call heads or tails to decide whether I was to arrest him or not. He was even more bemused, but slowly realised I was serious. I had already made up my mind I was never going to arrest him for this minor misdemeanour but I needed a get-out rather than just let him off which would have allowed him to think this was acceptable. He said, "What for?"

"Well" I replied, "to decide whether I arrest you or not"

"Huh?" He looked astonished.

"Yes, you know, you make the call and you either get arrested or not"

After a considerable pause, he eventually said, "Tails... no heads, ... no tails, no HEADS!"

"Are you certain Steven? Heads for I let you go, or I arrest you?"

"Oh I don't know… heads you let me go".

I tossed the coin into the air flipping it speedily and it flew through the air leaving fate to decide in Stephen's view and me willing it to allow me the get-out for Stephen and not to have to think of another reason to let him go. I caught it expertly, slapped it on to the back of my hand slamming my other hand on top. I looked at him, he looked at me and we both looked at the back of my hand… I slowly lifted my top hand… there in the sunlight glinted the 10 pence piece, and the side facing up was the head of Queen Elizabeth II.

"Good choice, old boy" I shouted, putting the pea-sized cannabis on the nail of my thumb and flicked it into the undergrowth. He let out a restrained cheer; I think he actually enjoyed the experience but more so when it was finished, he left with a skip in his step. Justice had been done.

4. What a Set-up!

In times gone by, it was a regular event to be a victim or a part of a set-up in the police by your colleagues, something that can so easily be thrown back now as bullying. It wasn't, it drew a section together, and when you were new in service, I found it very much a bonding experience. It would happen quite rarely and usually everyone was involved including the control room, a vital piece of the jigsaw.

I was buying a house in Torquay and it had not been a good purchase so far. I was aware the previous owner needed to sell and I needed it for the cheapest price as I simply couldn't afford anymore. A princely sum of £75,000 but it needed a lot of work, and to give you an idea as I would do all the work, I would have a cement mixer in my lounge for at least 3 months. I had never seen the previous owner, but I would get messages through the estate agent saying he wanted extra money for the carpets, so I said take the carpets, he wanted extra money for the garden shed, so I said take the shed and inevitably the carpets and the shed remained. It was a nervous moment once we'd agreed a sale, signed contracts but hadn't yet exchanged, so it would have been quite expensive to get out for me now.

I may have mentioned this to my colleagues when I was doing paperwork in Paignton police station which has since been levelled in the cut-backs. I didn't take much notice of the police radio call for a unit in Torquay to attend a noisy party in a road that I recognised was in the same road as my new house. I took more notice however when backup was requested but was relieved when I found it was number 7 and not my house of number 4. This changed rapidly however when the attending unit said, "Victor, I've just realised it's number 4, not number 7, the house number was upside down".

I thought, now come on stay professional and let the guys sort it out. Best I stay out of the way. I would be emotionally involved if I saw some strangers wrecking my new house.

"Victor from Foxtrot 3-0, can you request a glazier for the smashed front window. 6' by 4' in size. It's a large double glazed one".

I was out of my seat and sprinting towards my panda car that was looking rather lonely in the car park. The little wheels of the Ford Escort span (probably in my imagination) as I accelerated out of the car park towards Torquay, some 3 to 4 miles away.

"I have an interest in this property, Victor," I said. "I'm attending".

I know at this point the whole of Torbay were hoping I didn't "bend" the car on route to this job, but they knew I was now a 30 pound fish on the end of their hook! I sped on and listened intently to the updates... "Victor from Foxtrot 3-0, can you put on the log, a replacement car fire extinguisher is required for our car, and there was a small fire in the lounge we've managed to put out. It's quite difficult to keep control of these party-goers so can we have more units please?"

All sense of thinking straight was now gone. I knew what this man had done. Angry that I hadn't conceded to his demands for more money and feeling he was caught in a corner having to accept a low offer on the house, he had invited all his family and friends for a free for all at the house, "and don't worry if anything is damaged". All these thoughts went through my head… "How do I get out of this sale?" It's going to be expensive, but it's got to be the best thing to do'.

I swung my Escort around the corner into my new road address and saw a lot of full dustbin bags outside the house. "Blimey they've had a party" I thought. I slewed to a halt and jumped out of the car. I ran to the front of the house looking for the damaged window, there was none but it must have been on the back then. There was bunting outside the house so they'd made an effort. I worked my way around to the back of the house and saw nothing. "Strange" I thought and cupped my hands up to the glass to help me see inside dreading what was going to be revealed. "Actually, it's not as bad as I thought…" My words disappeared to a whisper as I was distracted to a noise to my left. There was my whole section in a group, clapping and laughing. "Bastards!" I exclaimed with the most relieved expression on my face. They slapped my back, laughed and went through every detail of the radio messages… I had been completely taken in by it.

"And the bunting?" I asked slightly confused.

"Oh we got that out of the property store," they replied. I had been well and truly set up and I loved it. That was a bonding experience for all. The control room staff enjoyed it as much as everyone else! I'm proud to say I was set up because it meant I had been fully accepted as part of the team, and I think it's something that is a shame that over-sensitive people have got rid of in today's world.

5. The Beautiful Couple

I got into work at 6.30am to start work at 7am. I was getting the section organised to see who was on what call sign. I had 3 Traffic Officers and 5 Armed Response officers who made up the section. Together we went to numerous Serious and Fatal Road traffic collisions and attended some serious incidents which made us a very close-knit unit. Obviously the Armed Response units were even tighter units having trained together and having attended many firearms incidents together. I started to put the names and call-signs in the computer deciding who was going to go with whom today. The weather had been awful with flooding all over the country. The night-turn Sergeant radioed me on a point to point, a private line on the radio with which we could contact someone without everyone else listening in. "Harry", he said. "I've been overseeing a search for a person who's been washed away in his car. Can you take over?"

I drove out to the scene near Exeter. I was driving carefully as there were branches and other debris strewn across the road. It took about half an hour and I reached the point of the road diversion. A lonely yellow sign with black print showing the alternative route: I could see the flood had backed leaves up behind the legs of the sign making a small dam, the flow of water still managing to rush past. The rain had died to a spit but the run-off of rainwater from the fields was still creating quite a flow. I slipped past the sign in my BMW police car and gently made my way further up the hill and down into the next valley. I pulled over behind a row of police cars and vans parked on the verge.

Walking down the steep country lane, I pulled my black police jacket in close to protect my neck from the cold wind. The branches from the tamarisk trees were whipping from side to side in the wind and it started to rain again quite heavily.

"Alright, Jim?" I asked a lone figure with his back towards me. I recognised his large frame and stance, his legs quite wide apart, his hands deep inside his pockets. He always looked ready to take on trouble though. He span around and looked at me, his face haggard from a night shift without a warm cup of tea. His beard had started to grow from the morning before and he had looked better to be honest.

"Hi Harry, thanks for coming mate. I'm knackered to be honest with you, been trying to find whoever was driving this car when it got washed into the river at the ford. The divers are in there now but we've had to hold the scene until they got here. We've been searching all the way down the river for any signs but as you can see it's flowing fast. He may still be in the car of course but that's still upside down in the water over there, can you see?"

I gazed down from this little ford crossing what has quite a deep stream flowing over it now. Wow, that must have been quite a force to push the car off the road and into the river. I could quickly see why no one had a chance of getting to the car. It was caught in an inaccessible part with a torrent of water rushing past and through it.

"We've got someone!" a voice shouted. I could see a police diver on a line holding what looked like quite a light-framed person from the car. Now we'll have an idea, they'll get the number plate too so that should help us a lot as no one has yet been reported missing.

The body is pulled to shore with the help of some other local officers and divers. The sight saddened and surprised me. She was an elderly lady, about 5'3" tall of a delicate frame. Her face was as pale as the foam collecting on the side of the river bank, her eyes still moist and sparkling. As with all bodies the soul had clearly gone. This was just the packaging for the soul within and once that had gone what was left rarely resembled a person to me anymore. Her clothing intrigued me. Very traditional, a tweed suit with skirt and jacket. She was someone with money and standards.

The undertakers removed her body and took her to the mortuary. I would go there in a minute to establish any further details which may have caused her death, although seemingly obvious and to see what other forms of identity she had. We never presume she has drowned of course. It would be a perfect way to get rid of a body so we still need to ensure all the evidence confirms the cause of death fits. I get into my car and start to pull away in a sombre mood. It's the beginning of December and I know that someone is going to have a terrible Christmas when we tell them about their mother, their grandmother, their sister. A violent death they will struggle to get over.

There's some urgency on my radio. "Victor from Delta Echo 2-0, we've found another one. A body of an elderly male further downstream. We are recovering him now."

I'm already a couple of miles away and it's a couple more whilst I try to process the information I've just heard. It's so sad at this time of year. I decide to go to the hospital where the mortuary is in Exeter and await the gentleman to arrive.

I eventually make my way into the mortuary to meet the second arrival and a sight I see will stay with me forever. There on two trolleys side by side were an elderly couple of similar size and frame. Considering where they had been found they were immaculately dressed and there was even her handbag laid next to her. Side by side, looking as though they were just about to sit up and walk away, but these two just as immaculately dressed, the male in his suit and his wife I presume was in hers. They must have been to an evening do somewhere. I have a discussion with another officer. We think the male was driving with his wife next to him in the car. They drive over the already flooding ford and the car stalls. They are now stranded in the middle of the ford so the male gallantly gets out of the car to see what he can do. At this point the water starts to lift the car having spilled over the car sills so it's now not only pushing the car, but maybe going inside of it too. If this man was still standing, he now has to watch his car with his dear wife inside being pushed into the river and away into the dark and unforgiving night, and he would have soon followed. I cannot think of anything more upsetting for both of them. Those poor, poor people and after they had probably spent most of their lives together.

With the details of some identification found in her hand bag, and the registration number of the car, I make my way to the address to see who is there. It's a small village the other side of the ford so they were clearly on their way home. I get to it at about 10am a well-kept bungalow with a private drive with no car in sight. There's a single light on in the lounge. I take a deep breath and ring the doorbell and wait. Nothing, so I knock loudly and still nothing. I start looking through the windows of the kitchen and then the lounge. There's a small fan-light window open in the kitchen so I jump up onto the windowsill, and reach in to open the larger window below. I climb in over the immaculate sink. Not even a cup drying on the side, but some pretty flowers in a pot on the sill I have managed to avoid knocking over.

I jump down onto the floor inside, have a look around and can hear a radio in the background. There's a small table set up for breakfast in the kitchen. A plate and cup with spoon and knife, a teapot and milk jug with the mirror image of the same opposite. Everything is clearly set up for two. Two people who have lived together and nurtured their routine over the years. I walk past the table and into the lounge. Again it's spotless and there are numerous photos on the windowsills and a piano sitting in the corner. A middle aged couple with two teenagers look at me from a silver frame. It has to be their children and grandchildren. There's a large highly polished mahogany table next to the piano and on it are rows and rows of meticulously arranged Christmas cards, each with an envelope with a fresh stamp attached. About 50 cards I estimate. I knew that none of those cards would be delivered this year.

The radio is on to fend off the burglars along with the single light to warn them of the possible inhabitants. It's a local radio news programme and the male presenter is shouting out the news headlines with a sense of urgency. He says something that sends a shiver running the full length of my body, from my neck to my heels when I hear as clear as can be,

"And police are still looking to identify the bodies of an elderly couple found dead having been washed from their car into a river during the storms last night."

Here I am listening to the fate of this lovely couple whose house I have just broken into and intruded on in their most private lives. It was a surreal moment that will stay with me forever. God bless them both.

6. Car and Foot pursuits!

Two Parson Jack Russell's, Copper and Polo are sitting indignantly in the back of my Pajero 4-wheel drive car as I trundle through Palace Avenue in Paignton. They are on their way home from the vets and are not talking to me. Both have had their yearly jabs at the vets and Copper has had a rather podgy finger up his bottom. I swear his eyebrows are still raised and he is refusing eye contact as I look at him in my rear-view mirror. Having caught a glance, he turns his head slowly away from me with utter disgust.

I had been in the Firearms Unit for 7 years and through a special deal with our clothing suppliers I had managed to purchase a khaki fleece that looked quite militaristic for the princely sum of £5. The relevance of this will soon become apparent as I say the next moment my attention was drawn to the sound of a very loud and automated repetitive voice shouting, "Call the police, this security van is being attacked, call the police".

Palace Avenue is a little bit like a very large roundabout with a green play area in the middle and as the roads convened the other side of this park I found the blue security van and myself were on opposite sides of the road. I could see a security man with navy trousers and pale blue shirt playing tug of war with the cash box he was tightly grabbing hold of. A man in his 20s pulling on it from the other side attempting to grab it off him. The security guard was wearing a helmet and visor which was repeatedly being whacked with a long metal bar swung by another male.

I caught this in slow motion as I got out of my car. Thinking of the best form of attack I surveyed for weapons but could only see a bar so that was good, I had a chance. I looked for police but there were none. Do I ring them, no time, is it achievable to do something, hell yes, I could get myself one at least right! I ran over and not being sure whether there were guns involved and being dressed in jeans and khaki fleece I may just have shouted, "Armed Police, Stop!"

I come to a stop just 10 metres from all three of them and all three of them stopped, turned around and look at me with a look of complete astonishment. There's a starburst with one robber making a dash for it but having to run between me and the bank itself. A vain attempt to do a hero trip spectacularly failed as he majestically avoided my secret foot sticking out weapon and so I realised I would have to concentrate my efforts on the main man. I thought I would stick with the man with the metal bar who was still with the guard. Realising his mate had abandoned him completely, iron-bar man makes a dash for it as well at full pelt with bar still swinging towards me as he passes. I give chase and as he sprints up through the centre of the main road and onto the pavement with shocked members of public jumping aside I tell myself I would rather die than lose this man. Not through duty or honour you understand but through pure ego I assure you. I couldn't allow this one to get away now. This is a big fish and I couldn't be that angler who allowed that champion pike to get away. I can hear the engine of a car driving behind me keeping a steady pace and I naively think, "Ah the great British public, one is following me to help". Little did I know this was in fact the getaway driver wondering whether to mow me down or hope I would soon give up so he could pick up his colleague. That was a little bit of a sobering thought afterwards.

I have invested everything into this run now and I was not going to let this one go no matter what. I have watched far too many wildlife shows to know the cheetah however much faster than it's gazelle quarry has to catch it within the first 200 metres or it's onto a sticky wicket. The psychological test is won by the gazelle as it silently laughs at the pursuing cheetah whilst jumping and darting over the large rocks and tufts of grass to its inevitable freedom allowing the cheetah to scowl in defiance whilst it attempts to hide its embarrassment.

100 metres already gone and I've got this in mind. There's only one thing to do at this point and it's never let me down. Deep breath and use my last oxygen for this very calm and controlled voice... "I'm caaaaattttttchiiing yoouuuuuu!"

It totally freaks them out as they wonder how the hell you still have so much control and composure and above all, oxygen. This inevitably leads to your assailant throwing their hands up in despair gasping, "I give up, okay I give up!"

Iron-bar man threw his arms up and shouted "I give up, okay I give up" and I threw him to the ground grappling him in to a wrist lock, being surprised how weedy he actually was but I guess that's what drugs do to you. The iron bar left his grasp and rolled along the ground settling at the foot of a very elderly man with a rickety walking stick. I glanced up at him who had shuffled over to me tapping me on the shoulder with his stick, "Well done son, well done indeed!" I could then relax a bit and smile but I immediately thought, "Oh Christ, my wife is going to kill me!"

"You always have to get involved," she said to me trying to hide her sternness. She hates it when one minute we are driving along to the shops or to see my mother in Newquay and the next I'm lying on the floor holding the head steady of a crashed motorcyclist we have wandered across. I know the truth of it is she's exactly the same and if I wasn't there, she'd see if there were others helping but if they weren't she'd be the first to help. She's worried I will bite off more than I can chew however, which is sweet. Maybe she'll be right one day but I just cannot bear some yob thinking they can get away with ruining someone else's day.

As I was on the Armed Response teams I immediately phoned my colleagues in Exeter giving the description of the van that had been following according to witnesses. Exeter lies at the gateway of the motorway leading into Devon and Cornwall and I knew they would keep a lookout for it if it were making a break for freedom. There was no such luck catching the others however but my chap got himself a sentence of 3 years in prison for his failed efforts. I do wonder if I had just released the hounds from the back of the car whether Copper and Polo would have bagged one each! Copper had a lot of frustration and aggression to release after all.

This does remind me of an incident that happened some years later when I didn't need my shouty technique. As a police officer you have to use what's around you and think outside of the box. I was 6 years into my service as a PC and was sent to a potential burglary at a campsite in Paignton. It was said the offenders were running with portable TV's towards the leisure centre having broken into a few static caravans. I drove my panda car into the car park and caught sight of a male walking towards me from the fields behind with a largish item in his hands. I stopped the car 100 metres away from him to look at him more carefully half expecting an innocent explanation. He looked at me. I looked at him. He stopped walking. He stepped two paces back and then slowly turned as if he thought if he did it slowly enough I may not even see him.

I started driving again at a quicker pace towards him and he dropped the item and ran. He ran fast and he climbed the grassy bank so I had to quickly abandon my car and pursue him on foot. Now usually as I was pretty fit and had a natural physique for running I could catch people. In fact given an equal chance I had never lost to anyone at this stage but hell, this guy was fast. He was now running full pelt along the main Dartmouth Road with traffic flowing past us. Here I was in black boots, heavy uniform trousers and navy blue Nato jumper (I loved those jumpers!) it must have been quite a sight for people to see what or who I was pursuing. Ahead was this young athletic fugitive keeping an equal distance and I was really concerned that this was the one I may have to give up on. I couldn't live with that or the mickey-taking that would have occurred back at the police station and all the 'what ifs' I would have felt.

My attention was caught by a bus driving next to me, called a Bayline Bus at the time. It was keeping a constant pace to mine. I looked at the driver as I was running red faced and gasping, and the driver looked at me... there was a lot of looking that day! And then the doors of the bus opened. I adjusted my direction but not my pace and jumped into the front of the bus. I held the bar and thanked the driver, caught my composure and said the immortal words I've always wanted to say: "Follow that man!"

There was a sudden round of applause from the considerably elderly passengers as they whooped and cheered. My work here was not done, and as the bus sped up I could see the running man glancing back, obviously feeling he had lost me. He must have had a sense of elation before his euphoria came crashing down to earth as I launched myself from the doors of the bus onto his back. It was everything or nothing and I succeeded in the former! He and I came crashing to the ground and after the "You're nicked" words came tumbling out of my mouth I sat down on top of him like the proudest Cheshire cat in Paignton! All became clear when we carried out a 'Section 18 Search' which is a search after arrest to locate items relevant to the crime. Amongst his items proudly displayed were numerous medals for marathon running. Suddenly, I didn't feel so bad. I now realised there was more than one way to get a result. I was learning fast.

Fast forward 10 years and I'm patrolling Exeter in my BMW X5 police car and I have a member of the control room staff in my passenger seat on a winter's night shift. It's good to get our police staff out into the front line to show them what happens at the other end of their radio messages and what actually goes on. Okay, it may be a bit of a day out for them, as well but consider for example they inform us there is a road traffic collision at Junction 29. I can now take the radio operator or call taker to Junction 29 and they soon realise we can attend the incident in ten minutes from our base if the collision is one meter south of the Junction. It would take another 20 minutes of high speed motorway driving (140mph) to reach it if it is just a couple of metres north of the junction. That's useful for them to know.

My passenger has never been in a police car so it could be either a rather exciting evening for her or rather a disappointment. At least she would know that it was often in the lap of the gods as to how busy it would be tonight. 10 minutes in and I receive a rather mundane call to attend a broken down vehicle on the main A38 in a dangerous position. I see the mouth of a junction just ahead of me surrounded by street lights so turn my blue lights on and swing into the junction to turn around. As I do so, a white BMW 3 series takes off like a scalded cat in front of me. "Strange," I thought, and accelerated with the belief it would pull over and let me pass but it continued at speed and now I realised I was in a pursuit.

My speed rapidly rose and I am scanning the pavements and junctions, the islands in the road and back at the car I'm pursuing. I inform the radio operator I'm in a pursuit and put the registration details through. I know they are working like beavers to find out why it is running from me as well as getting the helicopter notified and other resources to assist me. We approach a large roundabout with traffic lights but the driver ignores them. I slow to ensure people have seen me and then accelerate hard to make ground on the BMW. I see the brake lights flash on and the rear of the car raise up and then tilt hard to one side to turn sharp right into an estate. I'm now thinking, "should I abort, should I abort?" and "No, it's safe at the moment," I'm continuing to scan the pavements ahead and what traffic is ahead of this charging metal beast without thought or care for those going about their business with their families. I know I am relying on the offending driver to keep me out of court as at the moment if that car crashes and god forbid kills himself or someone else, I am in a whole load of legal pooh.

I am following my training, I am in control of my own driving continually assessing whether I can continue, then although I have exemptions for speed, keep left bollards and red traffic lights, the CPS will prosecute the poor officer for driving without due care and attention or dangerous driving. In law as time of writing, none of the training or experience of the officer can be taken into consideration when deciding how safe the officer was driving. The driving of a highly trained advanced driver with 20 years' experience is irrelevant and is compared to how my elderly mother is expected to drive. The officers driving should not differ from hers or any careful and competent driver in fact, so I am not insulting my mother! Therefore they argue that if the offending driver was driving dangerously then so was the police driver which is a ridiculous assumption as a police officer is taking a professional assessment of every foot of that drive whereas the pursued driver is running on luck a lot of the time and a deep urge to get away at all costs. Simply proven by the pursued running red lights at speed and the police officer slowing down even with a green light and using their skills to catch up again when safe to do so.

Sirens blaring to warn people ahead and blue lights flashing off the buildings around me I see the car drives into a cul-de-sac. There's going to be a runner in a moment so I warn the police control room who have already got the heli and dog en route. I pull back slightly in case the car suddenly decides to reverse back into me; a tactic to disable my engine by deploying my airbags and immobiliser or cracking my radiator whilst they only suffer superficial boot damage to their own. As I slow I see the car lose control and glance off the front wing of a parked Morris Minor. Indeed a classic car and one that I can only assume the proud owner is going to be furious about. The BMW then continued at speed, as if knocked off balance into the side of another parked car gouging a dent into the full nearside length of it, off another and then finally into the rear of another pushing it into the front of a house cracking the bay window with brickwork from top to bottom.

I come to a halt in time to see the driver of the BMW running at full pelt along the front of the terraced houses to the end and scrabble up onto the roof of a shed. Here we go again. Realising I have left the car with my rather startled passenger, door open, lights flashing, siren still screaming, I shout, "Stay with the car!" as I am aware there is a boot full of guns and I don't want the local oiks to have a field day by stealing a police car with a hefty bounty! The driver has now got pretty much to the end of the shed and is pacing away from me, dropping down into the rear garden. There's no way around it so I have to follow him weighted down with my body armour and QRV vest full of handcuffs, pepper spray, Taser, Casco stick, radio and torch. I look through the gloom as I gain my balance on the roof just in time to see my foot go through the corrugated roof of the shed, but it's too late, I am committed and I can now see the holes where he himself had just done the same. I manage to pull my foot out without too much trouble, skip across the roof as much as I can weighing like a small elephant and jump down after him who is now making off with great haste towards the garden fence.

I too jump down off the roof and continue my pace after him and see him dip down without warning and stagger forward as he unexpectedly stumbles into a garden fish pond in the darkness. If you've ever seen a dog running full pelt along a beach thinking it's running over some wet sand when in fact it's entering a deep puddle you will understand how it suddenly comes to an instant stop. It goes from full speed to an abrupt halt in about a meter of water. Having observed just this happen to the fellow I'm chasing, I do the exact same as I am quite close to him and have no time to react. He's out again and adrenaline is ensuring he's clear without so much of a second delay and up over the wooden fence in front of him. There is nothing for it but to follow, hoping I don't have an embarrassing fence fail. This is fast becoming like a scene from Hot Fuzz but I don't quite have the baulk to go through it.

We are now running along a path into some trees and I have absolutely no idea where I am. I am hoping either the helicopter can see me or the control room can see my GPS from my radio and call back-up. It's time, there is nothing else for it. 200m has now been and gone and I wasn't expecting something resembling a Royal Marine Commando assault course to cope with but there is no way I can allow him to get away now. Yes, so it's time... deep breath, my last breath and my old faithful technique that's never let me down yet. "I'm caaatttchhhing yoooouuuuu!"

It worked, totally freaked him out, confirmed by the fact he threw his hands up and shouted, "Okay, okay, you got me!" I had been expecting that line!

He fell to the ground so I drew my Taser in case he decided he wanted to fight me. He probably had a lot at stake of course, so I put my foot on his chest as he lay with his back flat on the ground with limbs out splayed. Taser dot on his chest, I stood there like a conqueror, my foe captured and disarmed. Okay, less of the theatrics perhaps I thought as I handcuffed him and led him back to the car... by a more civilised route of course.

The good news was he was wanted for a £53,000 burglary in Liverpool, was driving a stolen BMW on false plates, had other stolen plates in his boot and was wanted on warrant for failing to appear in court. The bad news was I had inadvertently pressed transmit when I shouted my 'I'm catching you' warning and now my secret was out!

One other thing I should point out. I went back to the car once I had handed my prisoner over to someone to assist with transport back to the police station. Sat in the passenger seat still and making no attempt to run, was a woman, the partner of the male. In the back of the car, was a baby only weeks old. If that car had rolled, they'd have thrown the book at me. This is why police nowadays are so hesitant about exposing themselves to the injustices of the law. Add an angry mother and family organising marches to protest against the evil police officer who killed her baby, and those that say the officer should have stopped, that nothing was worth the death of a baby, then politics just takes over. Hindsight should not penalise the officer. It won't be long before every officer watches criminals disappear into the distance having a free reign of crime. It's started to happen, and unless people wake up very soon and ignore these idiots who shout for justice with their biased agendas, often criminals themselves, then we shall reap what we sow. I spoke to Louise Haigh on the subject, the Deputy Policing Minister on the phone. She has since been very much at the forefront of the push for a change in the law, and it seems like she may just succeed.

7. Helicopters and Machetes

I'm double-crewed with Paul. A lovely guy who's working on my shift today from a different Section. We are short on resources and so it's a nice change to have a different Armed Response Officer with me for the shift. I'm the Operational Firearms Commander for the day so I'm in the car fully armed with the usual protection equipment including a Glock Pistol and a Taser. I have a G36 semi-automatic carbine and shotgun in the safe. We are having a chat putting the world to rights. He's a humorous guy and a pleasure to crew with and it helps he's pretty damned experienced too and someone you would be very grateful to have with you in a fight.

It's mid-afternoon and the call comes in from the Control Room. "Yankee 2-8, can you attend Holsworthy? There are numerous reports coming in of a violent male walking up the high street smashing car windscreens and shop windows with a machete".

"Received" I reply, "En route". Paul then taps in the destination into the SatNav and my heart sinks. One hour away from us going cross country and that's on the ragged edge. "Victor, where is my nearest ARV to it please?". Armed Response Vehicles are dotted all over Devon and Cornwall so if there's a big job, they often have to come in from various areas however usually one car can get there pretty quickly.

"Yankee 9-0? What's your ETA please?" Comms requests.

There's a slight pause and then a concerned voice returns with, "45 minutes".

I have to think fast, this just isn't good enough. I am going to have unarmed officers attending the scene arriving before us having to deal with this guy with only some pepper spray and an extendable Baton. I had to hurry things up a bit.

"Okay" I say, "Can I have NPAS (Police Helicopter) pick us up please?"

Comms get hold of them on the radio and they are already listening and aware. "No problems", they reply. "What's his location and we shall pick them up".

Ten minutes later Paul and I are equipped with a ballistic helmet, body armour, weapons slung around our chests awaiting the arrival of the police helicopter to pick us up. We've abandoned our police BMW X5 and we watch as the helicopter lands in a nearby field just 30 metres from us. Okay, I do feel a little James Bondish as we make our way towards it. We have an AEP (Attenuating energy projectiles) with us which simply put is a Baton gun. We have it with us along with Taser so we are fully equipped with a less lethal option if necessary as well as our usual more deadly firearms. Prepared for every eventuality you could say. We strap ourselves in to our seats being extremely cautious of things we are carrying that go bang. I've decided the stun grenades are safer left in the car safe. They wouldn't do a heli much good if they went off. We've practised this process in the past so it seems quite familiar. Ear defenders are on and we are soaring into the blue sky towards Holsworthy, a town in the middle of a lot of green area, it's extremely rural! It's still going to take 20 minutes to get there so I am intently listening to the radio from my earpiece under my ear defenders getting instructions from the Tactical Firearms Commander who is trained in firearms matters and gives the tactics to all ARV officers attending the scene.

The calls to control room about the violent man have slowed down somewhat and I'm worried the suspect has gone to ground but at least that means no one is being injured or worse at this stage. This could be tricky but I arrange a local unit to meet us at the local football pitch so we have wheels to attend the necessary RV area and hopefully deal with this miscreant quickly. I'm temporarily distracted by the utterly beautiful scenery below me. Farmland, woodland, rolling hills and valleys meandering through the landscape. I realise I am very privileged at this point. The clouds seemingly react to the hills, peaks and valleys below them, dipping, thinning and then billowing again. It reminds me how much of our country is still so green. It's noisy with a lot of vibration in the helicopter and I look at Paul. He's smiling and shrugging his shoulders as he clasps his G36 semi-automatic close to his chest. Two magazines are attached and the numerous golden bullets are clearly visible glistening like golden jewels. It'll be machete man against us and if we have to shoot him it'll be a 6 week inquest with several years of stress beforehand so let's see if we can avoid that shall we?

Every second of decision making and action will be meticulously analysed in court, pulled apart and thrown at me by top barristers being paid huge amounts of money. The media will explain how a cleaner with mental health problems was shot by police and he wasn't even armed with a gun. Those same would never wish to deal with him however. If he's swinging this machete from side to side with rage in his eyes and running towards me we will use a Baton gun against him with a Taser to follow up to gain control. That's the plan but we all know how plans can go, and if things don't go well, then ultimately I'm not risking my life for him. I don't care what any nine to five jury says. Better to be judged by 12 than carried by 6 as they say.

Damn, the radio has gone silent. There's no CCTV of course and I'm hearing he's disappeared. Good that he's no longer causing any issues but I still don't know if he's injured anyone or worse. The pilot circles around the town several times, dipping and diving to investigate possible suspects as if on a video game. The observer and pilot keep their eyes peeled towards a potential suspect walking down a nearby path, then darting over to the other side of the town to look at someone else, zooming in with their cameras. The enlarged images come up on the display in front of me. Incredible footage which enables me to see things in infinite detail. I see the benefit of being in this helicopter. I am covering so much ground and if we spot him, we can be dropped down pretty much next to him. We survey the town and there are several shops and pubs with smashed windows, so we bank over and the pilot skilfully drops the helicopter onto the centre spot of the football field. There's a police van waiting for us, so we jump out and jog over to the van.

We are taken to a nearby car park where I meet other local officers from Bideford to organise a search process. The other ARV crew turns up slightly later, its engine pinking and the brakes hissing. This car has been beaten up to get it here in time. The officers in their ARV gear nonchalantly crack open the car door, step out and wander over to me. "Hello Sarge, sorry about the delay".

Three hours later and we've searched 10 locations and addresses amongst us. We've clearly got the interest of the residents who are now updating Facebook. This could be embarrassing if we aren't careful. The town has been trashed by the suspect but fortunately no one hurt. We have a chat amongst ourselves and decide to have a briefing at the Fire Station. This is directly next to the Police station but quite simply, the Fire Station clearly has better biscuits. The local officers tell me about a number of houses with some of the 'underprivileged' in them. Christ I hate that term. It clumps together all those that genuinely have had a hard time in life through no fault of their own with those that couldn't care about anything or anyone and who make no attempt to improve themselves whatsoever expecting the world to pander to their every need. They are complete drains on society and some most definitely need a boot up their backsides to get themselves motivated. The welfare system protects these sorts of people. I see them every day. They are fit enough to deal drugs and burgle houses but not well enough to go to work.

We have a chat with a group in their 30s who've clearly rarely been sober in the past few years. I speak in a friendly manner with them and the conversation is civilised. There are a number of detached houses split into flats they live in. They assure us they don't know who or where this individual is and if they weren't so used to lying, I would almost have believed them. "Thanks, guys", I say, "We'll be off then, do let us know if you hear anything". I shouldn't have wasted my breath but you never know. As I start to walk back to the car Paul and I decide to search the rear gardens to the property. We split up as the garden is quite large and I make my way to the rear of what looks like an overgrown garden at the back of a house of flats. I suddenly feel my foot in a slippery substance and realise it's dog pooh! Just brilliant. I start to walk back towards the road scuffing my boot on the long grass to try to clear the sticky mess from my boot. I stop in my tracks, "Come on, Harry be professional" I think to myself so I turn back and make a special effort to walk through the tufts of grass and nettles to look behind a garden shed that's nestled in the corner next to the fence. If a job's worth doing and all that.

Feet, I see feet, yes feet. I can't believe it, and 3 minutes later the suspect is in cuffs and suddenly the day has just become so much brighter. Now how to get back to Exeter?!

Fortunately we get a lift back from the Response Inspector who came from Exeter who had arrived much later than us. He of course tells everyone he beat the helicopter to the scene I have since found out! We were just 10 minutes from returning back to our car with him when we get a radio call from comms. "Yankee 2-8, we urgently need you to attend east Devon where a courier has been attacked in his van with an axe". The day was still young and after a quick change-over back at our BMW, we were on our way.

8. Looking in the eyes of dead people

I was acting as spotter in Torquay for my Section on one of the few days we had relatively free issuing tickets for driving whilst using mobile phones, no seat belts, no insurance etc. These days were few and far between unfortunately but on this occasion I was enjoying the sun standing next to a bus stop on Torquay harbour-front in full uniform looking down at drivers in their cars to see if they were committing any offences. I would call the registration of the offending vehicle forward to the lads who were further down the road tucked behind the Princess Theatre where my prey would fall into their trap, often still committing the same offence.

I had tweeted a comment basically telling people where I was and that I'd just caught someone using their Ipad whilst driving over a pedestrian crossing! The answer came back from the Twittersphere. "You're just a tax collector for the Government".

Now when someone uses the forum of Twitter to have a go at a police officer I do quite enjoy it more often than not. It becomes a battle of wits. I rarely feel the urge to chastise or lose my temper. It is expected I should give some lecture on the irresponsibility of using your Ipad on pedestrian crossings whilst brushing your teeth and doing your nails, but quite frankly this is very boring and tends to just preach to the converted. I had a think and thought, a bit cheesy, but I'm going to go for it so I wrote...

"I look into the eyes of dead people, I'm no Tax collector".

I could visually see the silence... the Twitter audience awaiting the reply with anticipation and then it came. "Okay, fair enough". We had found mutual respect, and the world was good again.

Looking at the issue of road safety though is a big one. I have been involved with 'Learn2Live' for about 10 years where I present in front of students, those just about to drive or just becoming passengers in cars driven by their newly qualified friends. It's a cleverly designed process made up of part film part 'walk on' Police officer with a story of an event they've been through, then a fire-fighter, then a paramedic and a police family liaison officer, each with a tale to tell and then the mother comes on and talks about her dead child. There isn't a mobile phone screen shining in the whole theatre or school hall at this stage, quite an accomplishment for 800 students at a time. When a mother is standing there on the stage going through the time she was told about her 21 year old son dying as a passenger in a car, she's still holding his teddy bear he had when he was younger as she regales how she ran to the mortuary and saw him lying there cold and pale, when she then ran home again, climbed the stairs to his bedroom and climbed into his bed where she "could still smell him on the pillow". These accounts are usually local and studies have shown it to be an extremely effective way of teaching young people to empower themselves as a passenger to gain control of the situation if someone is driving badly or being distracted. It changes attitudes and convinces many a driver it could be them causing the death of their friends if they continue as they are.

My dear friend called Ali Norrish is a wonderful woman who has the most wonderful husband Mo supporting her and she is the mother of Anna, killed in a road traffic collision on the M5 just outside of Exeter in 2008. I was first on the scene to her collision where she had been instantly killed and where I attempted to save the life of the driver who was twice over the drink-driving limit. Anna was so against drink-driving but she took a lift believing he hadn't been drinking. The resulting situation was that Anna lost her life as did the driver along with the devastation caused to her family and friends; all those time-lines gone in life, birthdays, new jobs, marriage perhaps and children, all gone and simply because the driver convinced her he was fine to drive. I believe he fell asleep where he then crashed into the back of a highways truck parked on the hard shoulder. Ali has spoken about the death of her daughter Anna on Learn2Live for some time and ran an anti-drink-drive campaign, and it's interesting and devastating to see that when telling this account, she relives the events of that day in her mind each time, and the tears begin to flow once more. It's maybe slightly cathartic to talk about her daughter, keep her memory alive and crucially for her to help others, but it's also a journey she never wants to revisit either but does so to help others. Rest in peace, Anna.

9. A Road Collision

I'm attending a fatal Road Traffic Collision some distance away. I click into a different mode. It's time. Things are going to get very serious, you cannot let yourself or anyone down now and ultimately, someone has died and it's my job to save life if possible, but to then preserve evidence so an investigation can take place over time. I know that I or a colleague will soon destroy someone's life with the passing of a message regarding the death of a loved one. It's late evening and dark, weather good but the roads are wet, and I select engine mode 'sport' on the switch on my BMW X5 car console and then slam the selection stick across into sport mode too. The car lunges forward as if it were a large German shepherd straining at the leash. Before I put the sirens on I just apply the blue lights and I see the reflections bouncing off the nearby buses and office windows. The location of the collision is near Seaton in Devon and it's a 30 minute drive at this time but I'll get there in 20. I'm on the radio, "Local unit confirms one deceased yes?"

"Yes" comes the reply distinct and to the point.

"Okay" I reply, brain turning over six to the dozen. "Can we get a FLO (family liaison officer) organised and highways please?" This will stop any unnecessary delay with releasing officers and PCSO's badly needed elsewhere from the roadblocks that will have to be set up. It's very necessary to get the FLO there as soon as possible. It gives credibility to them when standing in front of the family explaining about the death of their son or daughter. They were there, they saw them, they were with their loved one and that's important to them. Why the rush to inform the family if they're already dead? I'd want to know as soon as possible if it was my son or daughter wouldn't you? It gives the FLO time to attend the scene, confirm the identity of the body and inform the next of kin (NOK).

As I'm driving, my eyes are darting all over the place, looking at the pavement for feet under parked cars, has that driver at the junction seen me, is that car moving out in front of me? My sirens send a crescendo of noise across my path in front of me scattering cars left and right leaving me a clear valley between, until one driver with either his stereo up loud and his rear view mirror adjusted to his passengers lipstick level, remains planted in the middle of the road. The penny eventually drops and the driver panics, continues on their way having jerked the car left and right but maintaining their obstruction still. It can't be a selfish action by them, I don't get angry over it. It must be a human reaction because so many do it on every immediate call I attend. If I'm taking a guest attachment with me they often exclaim in complete disbelief, "What the hell, why don't they stop or move over?"

"Good question", I reply. It surprises me how my passenger is chomping at the bit calling them all sorts of names and after a considerable time of this car blocking my path driving at 10mph in total panic with nowhere for me to pass, I eventually lazily wave through the windscreen at the driver and the car pulls over.

They just need to pull over slowly and stop in a safe place, but that's more than the brain can cope with sometimes. If the gentle request to pull over by the siren doesn't work, that melodic woh woh, woh woh, becoming mesmerising with little effect, the tap of the bull horn tends to do the trick. It's an aggressive intercity train sound, 'BAAAAAAAAA!" loosely translated as "F*** OFF!". It usually does the trick.

I throw my car into the bends of the countryside having escaped the town. I have to be aware of brake fade in these lanes, constantly accelerating and braking to and from an almost stop. After a tight left-hand bend the solid white lines blend into hazard markings which show me the road is going to offer me an opportunity to overtake, and as soon as the view opens up I've made my decision and I'm out and overtaking a line of traffic. Constantly checking my closing speed on the next bend ensuring I never take a gamble, never a risk. I drive like this on every working day so I can never take a chance as any risk-taking will inevitably cause me to run out of luck eventually in a whole career. I can never let that happen so I drive to 10% below the limit of the car and myself just so there's no surprises.

The updates are few and far between, I understand the ambulance is on scene and the Air Ambulance is circulating above the crash site. Another 10 minutes and I will be there. I ask the comms operator permission to have talk through with the officer at the scene. "Hi November 3-5, can you please just ensure you take registrations of any vehicles in the area that may be turning around and leaving and if you can get names and phone numbers of witnesses that would be great?"

My fear is those drivers may just leave thinking the police have enough witnesses but it's amazing how many you don't have at the end of an initial enquiry. I also want to know what the driving was like of the victim leading up to the collision. "Yes, he overtook me at a right stupid speed on the bend and I said to my wife, Christ, he's gonna kill himself". Those are the comments we need or indeed the opposite of that to show someone was driving sensibly and not taking risks just prior to the collision happening.

I draw up to the maze of flashing blue lights on the country road just after a right-hand bend. I don't want to drive over evidence and so I plant my car behind the main queue of local police cars, fire and ambulance cars. I get out, hearing the pinking of the hot engine. If a car could pant, I swear it would have been doing just that, the smell of hot brakes fills my nostrils. Now, compose yourself, back to being calm again, reflective on, body-worn camera switched to on and hat securely on head. I start to walk up the road and it's a scene out of the opening scenes of the TV drama Casualty. It couldn't have been edited better when I first see a fire-fighter walking down towards me. "Hi", I say and he replies with the same and we pass, then a paramedic hurrying down to his car. A number plate lies in the middle of the road, and a large part of the rear quarter of a car. A wheel and suspension arm has been trying to bury itself in the offside hedge. Oil is bleeding across the road in pools and I smell death. Yes, to me it's the sweet smell of differential oil from the axle of a car which is the telling sign that death is near, the main reason being it takes so much energy to smash an axle of a car to spill the oil that usually any occupants of the car at the time have very little chance of survival or if they do, they will be in an extremely bad way.

I glance to my left as I walk further and there's a car with minimal damage and then another behind with some more front end damage. Behind that there is the wreckage of a car that is unrecognisable. Twisted metal of carnage lies before me and inside one car on the front passenger seat I note the body of an occupant who's showing an expression on his face that isn't of a human. An expression the live occupant probably never pulled in the short 18 years of life, but now in one of death. The fire-fighters have done their best to extricate the body out from the jagged web of metal but it's going to take time. A doctor has called time of death and the emergency teams move on to others to help. We can recover the body later and concentrate on any other casualties who are still able to be saved. A small gathering of red and of green boiler suits huddles on their knees around a point of interest so I take a closer look. Paramedics and Air Ambulance medics are working on a male in his mid-twenties. He's wearing boxer shorts as his jeans and top have already been cut off. He is lying on his back with his left arm looped around the top of his head exposing his armpit where a tube is protruding.

He's got a collapsed lung and they need to get it re inflated quickly but the sense of urgency is frantic with tubes, oxygen bottles, defibs, syringes and scalpels being pulled out of bags and passed to the business end.

I know it's not looking good but these medics are incredible with what they do and they can usually work their magic for a positive ending. When it's this frantic though, it's not usually a good sign in my experience and unfortunately my experience in these things is far too extensive to be wrong with my premonition.

I spot the police officer who was first on the scene and have a quick chat. He's looking wide eyed and I can almost see the adrenaline surging through his system. He runs me through what he thinks has happened. A BMW sports car has been driven by the man they are working on and he's gone for an impossible overtake colliding with another car, fortunately just glancing off it but then totally losing it instantly killing his passenger.

A common story unfortunately. The registration numbers are run through the system, the insurances checked and we find the driver they are still working on is very well known to us mainly through misuse of drugs. This man has used his influence to show off to a young impressionable friend of his and ended up killing him. If he survives, the driver will have to answer why he had cocaine in his blood when he took the dangerous decision to overtake whilst having far less ability to take that decision. The frantic bustle stops and the weary medics stand up leaving a blanket over the body they've been working on. Okay, I think, that's two FLO's I require now.

Death messages are something I always preferred to do when I was early in my service even though I was quite young because I had had some experience in the death of my father and to be quite frank, I knew I was less likely to mess it up. I am not a FLO so this task is now left to my wonderful Traffic Colleagues who have often done well over 70 messages in their short careers. One officer told me having attended the scene of a dead motorcyclist, he was going to the parents' address to give the death message. He walked up the long garden footpath to the front door, took a deep sigh and knocked firmly on the door to see a very large-build man with a weathered face open the door. He looked the officer up and down and asked just one question the officer says he would never forget. "Which one?"

The reaction people have can be very different, and therefore it's very important we don't say, "Your son has passed" or "We've taken the body to the hospital". A loved one will hang on to any chance, possibility or hope they can. Passed isn't clear, and hospital is for sick people not dead so it's crucial more definite words are used, such as "I'm so sorry but your son has been killed in a road traffic collision. He is dead I'm afraid." And when asked where he is, the answer should be similar to, "He's in the mortuary".

I remember attending a suicide where the rider of a motorbike rode around a car park of a supermarket then stopped and very purposefully took his helmet off before riding around in a large circle again before riding at full throttle into the wooden lattice holding the earth bank up. There was no chance of survival and there was quite a mess to be frank. The supermarket had been informed there had been an accident so the store first aider was called to the scene. I can only imagine what went through the mind of the young lad carrying his little green first aid box when he rounded the corner and surveyed the scene which resembled a butcher's shop. I do hope they eventually got over it.

I attended the family home having learned he'd attempted suicide by jumping off a multi-story car park previously, but had somehow survived with horrendous injuries. He had been keen to succeed this time. There was no car in the driveway so I wasn't sure anyone was in. I may get out of this unenviable task after all however I was soon invited in by a woman in her late 40s and I asked her if she would sit down. After confirming she was his mother, I told her the news. She immediately stood up and staggered over to me still holding a tea towel she had come to the front door with. She grabbed hold of my police vest and hung on whilst collapsing her knees and began wailing like a distressed animal. She had just been told her son was dead and she had had to cope with years of turmoil with his mental health and now she knew it was all for nothing. She had lost. She would never see him again, ever.

There was the sound of the front door opening and assertive footsteps approaching the lounge doorway. "This is going to be interesting" I thought. A huge man filled the doorway in work gear, still wearing heavy dirty boots, "Well?" He asked, or perhaps making more of a statement, "He's finally done it has he?" He walked over to his wife and enveloped her within his huge arms, she sobbing uncontrollably, and he's staring into middle space whilst cradling her.

I feel so frustrated for those suffering the torments of mental health who have been left to cope with little hope for the future. Policing used to be 80% crime with a large part of your time out hunting for bad guys, drug dealers and burglars but all that has changed. It's 80% to do with mental health now, not based on any scientific data but my experience, be it missing persons or suicide attempts. It can take two officers off the street for the whole shift as the other agencies fail to cover their responsibilities, often through no fault of their own as they too have had the scandalous cuts to their budgets. I have seen weeping men begging for help, shouting to me on top of bridges telling me there is no help out there even though they beg for it, before jumping. You can imagine how that leaves me feeling. You can imagine how it feels when you run out of things to give them hope. You have to say that things will change, but many no longer believe that. That could be my son, or yours, that is unacceptable.

The buck stops here with the police. Any agency which cannot afford to fund 24 hours cover know the police will attend and supervise them until they are called in or turn up at 8 am. Two police officers from a city where there are only three more pairs of officers answering all calls. Two other officers will be on cell watch because someone is suicidal in the cells so they sit there with an open door all night. That's 50% resources gone from a city the size of Exeter and that puts a lot of stress and risk on to the remaining officers trying to deal with everything the night throws at them. How Theresa May as home secretary seriously thought she was doing the right thing astonishes me. I don't think she is particularly a bad person, but I think she's incredibly stubborn and naive to think selling the security locks on your country to save money was a good idea. It's a common theme for many influential MP's unfortunately to believe they knew best having gained advice from 'advisors' who haven't done a day's policing in their lives.

10. Taking the Fight to them

I have dipped in and out of the Public Order unit, not necessarily by choice but through the ebbs and flows of my career, initially as a PC when I wanted as much excitement as I could and later when I had to come out of Armed Response for three years on promotion to Sergeant. You cannot be in the Public Order Unit (PSU) and in the Firearms Unit as well because of the abstractions in training for each and the fact that both specialisms could be required at once. In Devon and Cornwall we probably weren't going to face thousands of marauding rioters demolishing everything in their wake in the town of Torquay or a city such as Exeter perhaps. Exeter is too posh to riot anyway or at least too well brought up! What I did find was having just qualified as a PSU officer with my huge bag of kit including overalls, pads and helmet I was immediately seconded to deal with the protection of the building of a dual carriageway bypass between Honiton and Exeter at a village called Fairmile.

There was a lead protestor who was very shy, dishevelled and to be frank, not entirely all that intelligent but what he did manage to be is a mole. His name was Swampy, and he was not someone who passed information when I describe him as a mole, but he and his colleagues dug tunnels, professional tunnels and then took shifts to hide in them so no bulldozers or earth works could take place above. There was a long and expensive standoff and I had just finished 7 nights of uniformed shifts when I was asked if I wished to assist with the policing of this bypass protest as part of a public order unit for the next 6 days which were due to be my rest days. In those days, that meant double time and therefore I was in to make a lot of money. We in the police loved Swampy and named many a conservatory after him!

Some clever thinking had to be done. The bosses met with the road builders and they both met with the representatives of the protestors but absolutely no ground was made quite literally. I spent the first couple of days standing on a fence line looking at the protestors jumping from branch to branch with their lines straddling branches high up in the trees but then the plan developed and we were called to a briefing in a large hanger. There was a large 3D model in the centre of the room I presume borrowed from the designers which showed the new road and countryside area around it, and there was also a Superintendent with a long pointing stick. The briefing began.

"Ladies and gentleman, we are going to attack their main base camp... listen in..."

The atmosphere changed to a silence like no other as I suddenly romantically transformed myself from a standard mundane police briefing to a war time bomber command unit briefing. But this wasn't about bombing a target deep behind enemy lines, this was the heavily defended main base of the protestors and I wasn't risking being blown up or crashing to my death; I may suffer a twisted ankle at best. Suddenly I came crashing back down to earth in a not so shot-down plane way.

The plan understood, we got in our Public Order PSU vans at Exeter Police Headquarters and a convoy of 20 vehicles left the rear gates at 10pm with all blue lights flashing. It was a sight to see as I glanced back through the dirty rear door Transit windows into the gloomy night behind. A sea of flashing blue lights which made the adrenaline surge through my veins reminded me of why I had always wanted to join the police. It was a team, a very big one. Our gang was always bigger than theirs. Everyone pretended it meant nothing to them of course as we didn't want to look like excited schoolboys, but we all knew this was big, but it could also go either way and be an unmitigated disaster and total embarrassment if we weren't very careful.

The order came for the blue lights to be switched off. They hadn't wanted to have Joe Public splitting the convoy up so the blue lights were used until we came off the main road. Then silence and after another 15 minutes driving, we pulled into the verge of a very dark country lane. Everyone got out of the vans in complete silence. The next part was crucial. It was benefits day and the intelligence had shown that on this night every week the camp had a skeleton staff of protestors to protect it as most of the others had gone to the local pub to spend their hard earned money. We were to be led by the local gamekeeper through the woods over prebuilt temporary bridges across streams and ruts right up to the main camp. Our Tactical Aid Group would be at the front with the long, wide metal ladders and they would put them up the sides of the defences and catch the sleeping occupants by surprise. We would flood in behind and get to the tunnels before they could to prevent them taking their defensive positions. There was a risk there was always someone down there in the tunnels but at least it would be minimal and fewer to negotiate with. Well nothing too exciting about all that then, especially for a young officer in his mid 20s!

The vans formed up in a long queue, two abreast. There was no light whatsoever. Not a star in the sky, and not a sound to be heard, even the wildlife was keeping its head down. We started walking and by gripping the person in front by the back of their collar, we could get the only reference possible to establish the direction we were to go and even get an idea of the terrain under our feet.

Having walked for approximately 10 minutes we entered a wooded area and the pace slowed. We had to move in single file on occasions and then spread out to two parallel lines again when things got easier. 'Bridge' was whispered to warn we were going over a small stream with a makeshift bridge built just for the occasion. The game keeper had built and placed wide planks across the streams to enable such a large body of men and women to get to their target... or should I say destination! There was incredible planning behind this and hundreds of officers were secretly extremely impressed so far. This continued for another 20 minutes or so but the discipline maintained throughout and not a voice was heard apart from the officer in front whispering 'Bridge' on a very few occasions.

Then out of nowhere the mood changed, something was happening up front. There was a lot of shouting and searchlights as though looking for enemy bombers in the skies above. Lights beamed out into the dark sky and scanned the tree trunks and mud bank walls of what we could now so clearly see was the main encampment. I could see the ladders of the Tactical Aid Team were already on the walls and the longest millipede of officers imaginable was crawling up the ladders, over the ramparts and into the base. The element of surprise was achieved. We were impressed, and if they were honest they were impressed too although a little embarrassed about being caught with their pants down. Mission accomplished.

I was quite busy in Plymouth with the veal export protests mainly lifting very elderly ladies out of a road. Not exactly what I envisaged when joining the unit, but then I was also used as part of a PSU angry man team for going into a house to arrest someone wanted for a violent offence who was standing off shouting he'd kill any copper that came into his flat. There were a lot of those and especially when I was a Sergeant in Plymouth. My whole 3 years there as a Response Sergeant was pretty much made up of smashing doors down of some quite horrible people. I was a believer that no criminal told the Devon and Cornwall Constabulary when we could arrest them by using threats against us. Other Sergeants would prefer to wait until the morning when the offender may have sobered up or got bored which was probably far more sensible short term, but I would order an angry man team in to do the job and to get the job done quickly but to send a strong message at the same time. This would involve a team of at least 3 officers with shields using a shock and awe tactic. It was small but quick and once organised anyone on the receiving end would think twice about taking that option the next time they faced being arrested.

I remember supervising one of these incidents in the depths of a particularly rough bit of Plymouth. I won't name it but let's say they still had a Ford Capri in the front garden of one of the council houses along with a small child standing on the street corner who looked as though he had got lost from a Plymouth Princess Theatre production of Oliver Twist.

There was a man in an armchair in the main lounge, sitting there with two large kitchen knives. An officer needed to speak to him over another issue and he'd unceremoniously told the officer to go away. So there we all were. This was a mental health issue where he needed assessing so we certainly had some empathy for his situation so we would ensure we got control without hurting him if at all possible. My team is ready to go but I need a legal power of entry. He's not threatened us in any way, he's not self-harming but he's acting very unpredictably and you certainly wouldn't approach him as he was. I shouted through the letterbox... "Mr Dawes?" but got nothing back. "I'm Sgt Tangye, what are you going to do if we come in and speak to you?"

The reply was loud and definite, "I'll shove these knives where the sun don't shine, Sergeant".

Respectful I thought, but that would perhaps give me my power of entry but extremely weak I agree, but then something developed that gave me an even better power. "Sergeant!" one of my PC's shouted. "He's set fire to his footstool!"

I took a glimpse through the window and the fire had quickly taken hold engulfing the foot stool at the very real risk of spreading to the rest of the house and the man with it. We had to go in fast and I shouted to the team, "Go, go, go!"

The officers smashed the front door of the house using the 'big red key' a heavy battering ram which does the job, splintering the wooden door into firewood. They were in in seconds. I put my head into the doorway to establish what progress was being made. I was aware I had another couple of Response Officers behind me and as I focused into the gloom my eyes widened with alarm because coming towards me at great speed was a large Public Order officer running at full pelt with a huge foot stool on fire gushing black toxic smoke and flames above his head as he ran. I shouted at the top of my voice for all to hear, including the semi-hostile neighbours who'd been slowly taking an interest from their house boundaries.

"WATCH OUT, THERE'S A FLAMING POUFFE COMING OUT OF THE HOUSE!!"

Now, to think my career was over at that point could have been an understatement. I was now praying the chap in the house wasn't gay as I'm not sure many would have believed the coincidence. The blood drained from my face until I was soon relieved by scanning my eyes around to the not so hostile neighbours anymore who were now sniggering bystanders and then to the belly-laughing officers laughing so loudly having forgotten the flaming pouffe was now setting fire to the nearby fence. More laughter and a rather bewildered but safe detainee being led from the smoky house just summed up to me how incredible this job can be sometimes.

Then there was football of course. The Plymouth Argyle matches could be interesting to say the least depending who was down to play them. Some had reputations for yobbish behaviour of course but most were okay generally. I am not a footballer, I'm more of an Exeter Chiefs Rugby fan as they are top of their game and, well you can drink beer in the stands, there's no fighting and the participants don't tend to fall over in agony over an inadvertent rub from an opponent's finger. Well that's all those clichés completed but it amazes me how different the two games are even though the main concept is for one team to get the ball through their opponents to the other side.

Saying all that however, I did very much enjoy running a public order unit at some football matches. My orders were to ensure any supporters coming out of the East Gate did not get through to the other side where they would mix with the local supporters. My Public Support Unit (PSU) were now the line that would enforce the separation between the two teams and my last orders I heard from the PSU Inspector was, "Harry, whatever you do, do not let them through or there could be carnage and we may not be able to recover it".

Forty five minutes later I get the message that supporters have broken through to rush our point. I hurry my men through to get to the position we've been allocated, fling the door open from under the grandstands to the outside area and lead them out to the location we need to be. Nothing but empty space thank goodness but I confess I was slightly disappointed as well. I order them into position and listen to the frantic radio messages in my ear, but I'm looking at a very bland concrete corridor outside the main grandstand... but then, oh my they came and they came.

I push through my team and shout "HOLD POSITION". I have the Inspector's orders ringing in my ears from half time, but this, there were hundreds of them! We could be absolutely annihilated but by hell we were going to go down fighting like Vikings. I wracked my Casco Baton, its glistening metal extending bar sending a message to the huge mass of angry men in front of me I was here to stay. I could hear the snapping sound of my officers' Cascos doing the same behind me. We were a team, and it was going to be tough but at least we would be remembered for going down fighting. I shouted at the baying crowd who to my surprise stopped dead in their tracks. They were staring towards me with a certain look of fear in their eyes or at the very least, uncertainty. I took the upper hand and shouted, "GET BACK!".

A huge group of very angry men took a hesitant step back. This is truly amazing, we must look so formidable, the sight of 8 men in boiler suits with helmets was enough to strike fear into their hearts...

our confidence was like nothing else. The crowd started to gain some confidence and stepped forward again, fists raised and clenched, red enraged faces shouting abuse and threats, so I shouted again and they hesitated once more. I eventually glanced back to ensure my men were still in position, looking strong and steadfast. I knew they would hold fast but I saw something else too, something that amazed me and froze me in position for a few seconds. What I didn't expect to see was a formidable body of 20 huge public order officers with shields and Batons raised, visors down ready for action. The lead one said calmly, "Harry, impressive mate, but do you want to get behind us now?"

I was both relieved but a little deflated too when it dawned on me that it hadn't been any of our actions that had stopped the wave of violent yobs, it was the other 20 from the Tactical Aid Group that had been there all the time, wondering what the hell eight officers thought they were doing trying to stop a huge angry crowd in front of them, but this hurt ego soon turned to a giggle, I was giggling like a child and the relief of the whole situation came rushing through all of us as it dawned on us. We thought we had been David against Goliath when in fact there were a hundred Davids with slingshots poised standing behind us all the time! I had forgotten this tale until recently when in the armoury at Headquarters and one of those Tactical Aid Group officers who is now a force armourer some 20 years later reminded me. "You were going to go down like fighting Vikings, weren't you!" He chuckled with a beaming smile on his face. "Good times Harry, good times!"

11. Night-Time Economy

I have spent many hours of many nights working on Night time economy. That is dealing with drunks spilling out from the night clubs when most other tax paying members of public are in bed asleep to preserve their energy to go to work the next morning. I have been guilty of being part of this drunken group on occasions but am very much on my best behaviour at least attempting to look remotely sober. Others really don't care what they look like and as soon as they hit the fresh air of the night and see a police officer, think this is just the time to pick a fight with someone as they know full well we will stop it from progressing further.

This tactic is the epitome of cowardice by the drunk who's lacking attention in his sober life so it's only polite and serves due justice to take a little time to render them assistance if they inadvertently pick on the wrong person who is taking none of their behaviour and very much getting the better of them. Not enough for them to get hurt you understand, but enough for them to look willingly towards us with the "Okay aren't you going to save me now?" look.

There's a whole psychology I have witnessed with night-time policing. The wheel goes round where some boss decides they want as many police on the streets as possible to show force and prevent crime, and before you know it, every officer is tied up with prisoners and there is no one to attend the other emergencies in the city. Having worked in Plymouth and Exeter, by far the best tactic is to be very nearby with reinforcements available but not necessarily in sight with a skeleton staff and CCTV covering the marauding herd of drunken wildebeest roaming the streets. The reason for this is there are enough police dotted around to put off serious crime but not enough to stand around chatting about nothing in particular which often results in no one leaving the area. The police just by being there create a social circle for the public to gravitate to. The end result is no one goes home for another hour at least, especially if it's neither cold nor wet. If they are hanging around it doesn't take long before someone has looked at someone the wrong way and that's 4 hour's paperwork to do when it ends in a bundle and someone is arrested.

My tactic was to pack everyone up at the end of the night in the police vans and drive off around the corner. We would wait for CCTV to inform us of any public order but inevitably the merry crowd disappeared into taxis or meandered into the side streets and soon there were none left. A new Inspector who wanted to make a good impression to their Superintendent would then come on the scene and we'd go back to square one, standing outside clubs until the last person had gone and strangely enough there were many more arrests because of the congregating and the overtime spending inevitably rose.

The most usual drunken comments were things such as, "I've got a criminal record right, a GBH and a Burglary, can I get into the police still?"

"I know I've had my problems with the police 'cos I was nicked by this right cock of a copper, but I reckon most are okay."

"That doorman has kicked me out of the club for nothing. Can you tell him he has to let me back in?"

"Those twats in that club have refused me entry and I've done nothing, can you tell them they have to?"

The only expressions in response to these comments tend to be blank ones. On one occasion, I had spent a couple of days away on a Royal Visit working in my other role as VIP protection officer. I had been within 2 feet of Her Majesty the Queen on several occasions during her visit and of course my attire would be a very smartly pressed lounge suite with shiny shoes and with beautifully presented high powered cars for our transport. Here I was on my very next shift watching a rather huge 20 something spilling out of the door of a club on one stiletto, smudged lipstick up her cheek, eye makeup now performing a role more of that of foundation which may all be forgiven if it hadn't been for her being dressed in what I can only describe as a bikini than that of an outfit. Most of her body fat spilled over the material making up the top and skirt thus giving the impression of near nakedness which made for the choice for me to look away or study in a form of morbid curiosity.

As I am watching this, I smile at the difference between my roles in less than 24 hours, only to be emphasised with the woman slumping to the pavement having now exited the chip shop, but now abusing every passer by calling them all sorts of things I will spare you. I just hope she doesn't call someone a racist name as that's a whole different kettle of fish and that would be me written off for the rest of the night. Her chips and

97

cheese jettison across the road and she's now balancing on her extremely large breasts with her unflattering thong slicing through her bum cheeks on full display for everyone to see.

She's somebody's daughter I am thinking, I'm also wondering how she stood in front of the mirror earlier in the evening and thought, "Yes, I look hot tonight". Each to their own I suppose and if you think I should feel bad about this I don't. I don't because she has no idea I am thinking this about her so what she doesn't know doesn't affect her.

The next task is to either find a willing taxi to take her home or to find a friend or colleague in a rather better condition to take charge of her. To arrest her for drunk and incapable or drunk and disorderly is an absolute no no if at all possible. Custody won't take her in case she chokes on her vomit and of course that would be the Police's fault and heads would be demanded for years. She would hold no responsibility towards her own actions of course so now instead of arresting her, she's off up to casualty where two officers will now remain with her for the next 3 or 4 hours as quite rightly she wouldn't be considered a priority. If we were to leave her in casualty and she left, then again, we would be held responsible. I could not afford to lose what is sometimes a third of the available police response for the city by having 2 officers stuck at hospital for hours on end. The end result of this of course is that officers are naturally taking more abuse if they wish to get home and not ruin their next day with their family. Quite frankly, not acceptable and only having extra officers will fix this. That is the only main factor in bringing some sort of order back onto the streets.

It's always rather amusing when some delightful member of public having consumed their tenth pint of beer on top of pre drinks decides because I won't take him home instead of him paying for a taxi he is going to complain about my attitude. This would be after five minutes of polite refusal carefully explaining why, followed by another 5 minutes of rather firmer, "You need to go home now" to "If you don't go away now, I will arrest you and take you to the cells, not your home".

The usual demand for my collar number takes place and depending on my mood I am in is whether I play about with them or not. As my collar number is clearly displayed as 3908 on my chest and arms, I sometimes verbally mix them up a little to see if they notice. "3098" I say and they drunkenly repeat it and then again even more slowly and slurred. One I remember after a pause asked politely, "Have you got a pen please. I want your collar number so I can complain?" My reply was polite but firm, "Why should I supply you with a gun to shoot me?"

I was however extremely impressed with some yob I had assisted in the arrest of after he had been found shouting in the street after a drunken night out, had refused to go home, had described me as a woman's nether regions and was locked up in the police van cell. Okay, I'll come to the bit I was impressed with in a bit. He then proceeded to spit phlegm at the plastic sheet covering the metal bars to protect the officers in the van from such behaviour and repeatedly declared he was going to kill me within 48 hours. He later shouted he was going to kill himself in his cell that night so realising the maths of the two threats did not match up, I was even less concerned but I knew he had talked himself into a strip search and a paper suit as any suicide threat dictates.

Such threats to kill me hold no concern as I and every officer hear these often and most of these little oiks couldn't get out of bed in the morning let alone think up some killer plan. It doesn't mean they shouldn't have the book thrown at them, mind, as it's still not pleasant and they are completely disrespecting the uniform of Her Majesty's Police Service and once an acceptance has been made for this behaviour it's a slippery slope but I suspect we are well en route down that slope already.

Before CCTV and mobile phones I suspect the subject would have slipped as they were assisted into the police van which meant they were not so derogatory to the officers the next time. I don't feel that was such a bad thing as now there is simply no respect at all for the authority of law and if anyone is to be hauled over the coals it's usually the officer as the criminal knows they simply need to complain about some fictitious incident and the officer is in for a whole host of stress for many weeks. This is even if the officer is shown clearly on CCTV not doing what the accuser says he did. Things are bad on the complaints side of things, and several officers over the years have ended their own lives over them because the stress becomes too much, their careers are halted for years as they are not able to apply for promotion or different departments they've been aiming for, for so long. The whole process is just so unjust and now I expect to fight with every prisoner I arrest instead of so rarely in the past because put quite simply, there is no extra sentence or punishment for struggling against an officer. It's expected and accepted by those who don't have to leave their office chairs to do the bloody job.

Okay, the bit I was impressed with, and I hear you say, it better be bloody good now, was that this oik demanded my collar number and as he was in custody I had given my correct one to him. I thought in his drunken state there was no way he would remember it as on this occasion I hadn't been the arresting officer so wouldn't be on any records and as he was in custody, he wasn't permitted such a dangerous weapon as a biro. He had repeated my number like a mantra as he was led down to the cells.

The following day I was checking my emails and found the interviewing officer had sent me a photo. The photo showed a polystyrene coffee cup torn up into many little square pieces. They had been formed into shapes on his cell floor, and those shapes made up the number... 3 9 0 8.

Incidentally, there was no complaint. He probably woke up in the morning and thought what an absolute idiot he had been and as I can assure you, I am very polite and fair during my shift but I am not here to be insulted and abused and it gripes me when so many officers seem to think that's part of the job.

There are the surprises from time to time too. Exeter is a beautiful city with a very large student population. It's a vibrant modern city and much money has been invested into it. It has a beautiful quay area where you can walk or row down the canal to various pubs and quality eating places. Its cathedral is stunning where students and tourists love to mingle in the sun in the green area around it surrounded by restaurants, shops and cafes.

I was driving at about 2am through the city and I saw a male obviously quite worse for wear urinating in the street. This will be the attitude test quite frankly. I shouted at him. "Oy, put that away! What would you say if I went for a pee on your doorstep?"

His reply was in a very upper class tone, " I am so sorry officer, really, what a frightful thing, I do apologise. I shall go home immediately. Apologies once more officer!".

Now why can't everyone act like that? Policing would be so different!

And then there are those that are so drunk they wish to debate the fact they are not drunk and can legally stand around arguing with a very bored officer as the officer is his servant and the officer can't do anything about it. These are usually the ones who pick on some local who doesn't take so kindly to their debating request which usually ends up in a fight of some sort, and after several polite warnings the only other step before arresting them and wasting hours of police time, tax payers' money for very little result, is to spin them around by the shoulders and start pushing them up the street with the most authoritative voice I can muster, "Go now, and keep going, and if you come back, I will arrest you and you will be fined" and whilst their protests emit from a half stumbling drunken youth, I shout, "Not interested, Go! I don't want to see you again young man".

At this point I turn around and go back to where I have come from. This has the effect of either the drunk male having one last word before wandering off in a drunken state or returning for more and being arrested.

Then there is the well-meaning but rather naive and ill-informed drunk student of law who is in their first year who proclaims to me extremely assertively that what I did was illegal and I cannot push the drunk up the road and... and... and he refuses to listen to polite explanations as he assumes I don't know what I am talking about being a common cop and that he has caught me out in the middle of abusing this British citizen's rights. So it has to go up a gear...

"My dear chap, it is commendable that you try to defend the drunk man keeping the locals up, causing the tax payer to pay more in overtime for the file I will have to do if he is arrested, commendable that you have stood up against the fascist route of all evil and bravely confronted the corrupt officer but this isn't college. It is clear you haven't got to the page in your law books which contains the public order act or even more so, Section 3 of the Criminal Law Act".

I then spout the act verbatim as such, "A person may use such force as is reasonable in the circumstances in the prevention of crime and in the effecting and assisting of the lawful arrest of offenders or suspected offenders or of persons unlawfully at large"

The relevant part of this act being the "using such force as is reasonable to prevent crime". Having observed the "I've bitten more off than I can chew" look on the poor chaps face, I continue,

"A little knowledge is dangerous, my friend, and if you wish to carry on in your course with the intention of getting yourself a career in law, you really do need to walk away and google the said act I have mentioned. I do not have an hour for each student wishing to debate the rights and wrongs of civil rights and as an officer having done this job for 25 years, I know my stuff, I know my law and I know what I am talking about". Slight pause for effect... "Good Day!"

They usually wander off muttering at this stage. Until everyone has talked to a drunk student who believes the world needs changing and they are the ones to change it here and now, and if you just talk nicely to people they will be nice back, then they cannot understand how frickin annoying these rather naive and arrogant few people can be. Fortunately, the other 99.9% of students are an absolute pleasure. You can be polite for so long before you realise you will be there for an hour at least trying to convince them to do what you say and you really aren't a police state denying them their human rights.

I don't blame them of course, I really don't. I blame the school system, forced by the lack of support that has lost all discipline within its walls so that every student has a voice and should be listened to, their demands should be taken care of and any insults and abuse against teachers put up with from the very youngest of ages. The very first time they reach an authoritative figure that says no and actually means it, is when they are drunk leaving a club at the age of 18 years old. They shout, then they gesticulate, then they fight, and they blame the nasty police officer for police brutality. No, they have just never been taught respect of others, by their parents or teachers because they aren't permitted to quite frankly and they just don't know how to behave in an adult civilised society. Before you think I am anti-student, my daughter is one, and I have been taking students doing their Duke of Edinburgh's Award for the past 35 years to the Lake District and Dartmoor, and I know how wonderful so many, many students are. It reminds me there are others of that age other than the rude drunk bunch or those that feel they know better than the downtrodden police constable. There are some really very lovely ones too! I was just having a rant, okay?

Because the police service suddenly found they had no money after all the cutbacks brought in, they thought it might be a very good idea to put response officers, traffic, Armed Response and dogs together in one happy Section. This would mean everyone would get to know everyone and professional relationships would grow and the end result would be that it would save money somehow.

This system was called BluePrint and I was requested to be on the consultancy board as an experienced ARV officer to assist putting it together. Now I decided a long time ago not to go for promotion. I realised I was happy doing what I was doing and there was plenty to stretch me going sideways as opposed upwards. I didn't want to be stuck in an office and to be honest I don't think I would have been very good at it anyway. So whilst the Superintendent was trying to persuade me to join them, I politely declined as I knew this would take me off the streets and away from the role I loved. The Superintendent asked if I would do it part time, and I politely refused again explaining why and then he said, "What if you come into it now and then?"

I don't know how I maintained my constant refusal against a high ranking officer who was getting more and more frustrated but thank God I did because the whole process of BluePrint was a total disaster from start to finish.

The reasons were simple and experience would have shown why but there were too many people wanting to use it as a promotion step so they were adamant it was going to work or at least would make it look like it worked. The whole section was run by two Sergeants and an Inspector. An ARV Sergeant and a Response Sergeant on the whole and my Section worked well but there was a lot of resentment. The response officers couldn't understand why the ARV and Traffic Cars drove around all night and were never seen when Response officers were so busy and needed more people to assist them. Why couldn't they help? The Inspector who was in charge of a larger area but whose main point of stress was the City of Exeter tended to side with them on this.

This sounds quite reasonable until you realise the Dogs, Traffic and ARV officers were attending jobs with officers who were in the sparse rural areas and who so badly needed them. It was often a couple of officers covering a huge area and they were extremely grateful to see the cavalry turn up evening the odds somewhat. The ARV, Traffic and Dogs were attending serious and fatal RTC's all over the Force including Firearms Incidents which, because these incidents were run on different radio channels, the Inspector and other response officers were not aware of them. Resentment on both sides set in and it came to a head when a traffic and ARV unit had spent 6 hours at a fatal RTC in North Devon, had assisted removing the dead young woman driver from the car and escorting her body for continuity to the mortuary. Following an hour and a half drive back into the City, the Inspector who'd had a busy night dealing with clubbers berated the officers for not being around to help the city units at pub kick out time. I won't go into what was said next but not all of it was completely professional. Officers were getting stressed.

The Inspectors drove the Traffic cars even though they weren't advanced drivers, using them as pool vehicles which seemed reasonable until the knocks and scrapes appeared, the cars needed fuelling, they were left unclean, the pride of the unit diminished. The Inspectors and higher up bosses knew little about Traffic or ARV. They had never been to a training session, didn't know officers had to be available to

107

attend these jobs, to help local response officers and that guarding a cell or looking after a mental health offender in hospital probably was not the best place to keep your last resort. Resentment, and I think familiarity bred contempt, and it soon fell apart as a system.

It taught me how important it was to have a reasonably high rank in charge of every specialist department who had previous experience working within it. How old fashioned I hear some claim. Experience? You don't need experience! But you do, you do so you can bang your fist on the table to protect that department from the vultures who want to thin it down for their own means, who want to cut the department back without knowing the detrimental effects this would have. Experienced bosses would have realised the staff left would soon fall apart due to the stress and overwork with fatals for example. Of course austerity left very little choice for Chief Constables with this anyway. There was simply very little choice as cuts had to be made so I am glad I was a mere Sergeant and am not involved in those strategic decisions. The whole thing was a mess but we were fortunate in our Force to have a great command team who minimised the pain as much as possible. They never threatened, never said, 'like it or lump it' like some other Force's Command team did, they weathered the storm and they did good.

12. Wives, Dogs and Children!

As a 21 year old with a salary of £8000 I sold my very old beige Ford Cortina Mk 4 and took a loan out at 25% to buy a Burgundy BMW 318i with a discrete rear spoiler on the back. I bought a windsurfer and learned fast in the bay of Torbay and it just so happened to make the car look amazing too! The only thing missing was an attractive girlfriend to fit my new trendy lifestyle, but I had had awful trouble with acne for a couple of years so it had completely sapped my confidence. Policing now filled me constantly with self-doubt. Was I good enough, was I a fraud? Maybe my concerns were brought on by suffering from my very bad acne, a terrible skin condition which decided to hit my life once again, when I had joined the police. My acne had disappeared for a couple of years giving me a false sense of security as I was growing up and I believed at the time I had seen the last of it, but here it was again. I remember waking up every morning and despairing at the sight in the mirror. I was washing with 'Oxy10' which smelt quite toxic and seemed to have very little benefit either.

I did learn to hold my own when a low life laughed at me during a stop search saying, "Jesus, look at that acne, just out of school?"

Remembering a certain comment by the great Sir Winston Churchill, I said, "My dear chap" (I always get a bit posh when I am vexed), "My dear chap, whereas my acne will eventually clear up, you are stuck with your fish face forever". I had won the verbal battle and my pride was restored.

I watched my colleagues in single quarters go out and meet girls. Being a cop was quite attractive to girls and they did very well. I on the other hand, with my severe acne didn't have the confidence to chat girls up, how could I when I was so disgusted with myself. I went to the doctor expecting to be brushed off and to my surprise he changed my life instead. He referred me to a dermatologist who prescribed a drug called Roaccutane.

I have since heard some terrible side effects regarding this drug, including tendencies to feel suicidal. I wonder how much of that was from having the confidence beaten out of you with having ugly pus welts on your face for so long, because the only expected and guaranteed side effect I received was my lips became so dry they had the texture of a leather saddle bag abandoned in Death Valley. I should point out the drug could destroy your internal organs too so I had to have regular blood tests to ensure I still had a working liver but I put that down to a very small possibility and I was happy to take the risk, after all I wanted girls and maybe a liver was a small price to pay!

I was told I had to wait four weeks before my skin would clear to almost normal. I didn't believe it for a second of course. Just four weeks? I am sure my chemist thought I had an addiction to lip balm because I couldn't get enough of the stuff. The sebaceous glands in my skin, the glands that produce sweat were being reduced in size with this drug and four weeks later you couldn't have met a more exhilarated young constable as me. That was it; I was going on the town! I remember many a time seeing some poor chap covered in spots in his 20s walking along the road and had to fight the impulse to rush up to him shouting, "Hey, I can solve all your problems!" I passed the information on to my brother who is forever indebted to me as he had suffered from the same problem too.

Once my skin cleared up my confidence went through the roof and at 22 years old I was a police officer on independent patrol. Everything had come right and I was enjoying life. I was just missing a girlfriend to match my BMW and Windsurfer and yet this was soon to change. One very dark, late shift I was double-crewed with a wonderful friend and colleague Special Constable Vernon Savage. He was a contagiously funny and skilled Special Constable and later, radio operator who used the most beautiful language be it asking how myself and my wife were, or on the airwaves dispatching units. Everyone knew when Vernon was on the radio. It was a joy to work with him and he was one of the funniest and yet most respectful people I knew. He was musical to listen to but he was a very large man and didn't care for a healthy lifestyle. I was devastated to find he had died in his middle age.

It was when I was with him driving up Abbey Road in Torquay in my Police Ford Escort on patrol when I glanced across to the Abbey Fish Cafe to my right. My eyes became transfixed towards a vision of absolute beauty. There was a girl in her late teens with a seductive flowing figure. She had the most striking tanned smooth soft skin that looked like it had been dipped in gold dust giving off a subtle shimmer. She was wearing a tight green vest and skin tight snow white jeans; this description sounds strange now, but she was extremely infectious to look at as it showed her alluring form off beautifully. Her long slender neck was supporting model like features, her dark brown eyes beaming out into the world with the most attractively captivating shy but welcoming smile. I knew I had to find out who she was so I stopped the car and I looked at Vernon. He burst into nervous activity, "What have you seen, Harry?" He's spinning his head around to find the running youth I had spotted, but there was none. He turned around again looking at me completely confused at my odd behaviour, "What's a matter, what have you seen?"

"I need to do something", I said, as I reversed the car back down the hill to the large cafe window. It was dark outside and the lights shone from the cafe brightly. The activity in the cafe with customers queued up and clambering around the counter buying their fish and chips blurred out into nothing as I fixed my gaze on the girl standing behind the counter. "One day, Vernon, one day she's going to be my wife".

And one day she was, less than 18 months later to be precise. She was 19 and I was 23 and I married her, she having just won the title of Miss Torbay. Yes, I had done pretty damned good and I have the dermatologist to thank for that! We now have twins, a boy and a girl strangely enough both 20 at the time of writing and I am as proud as Punch for what they have accomplished. We immediately bought a house; you could do that then when they were less than the cost of your soul. I remember deciding whether we should spend our money on a small holiday or buy a carpet for the lounge. Needless to say, we didn't go away for 5 years and I often had a cement mixer in the lounge whilst any funds went on DIY projects. I was keen to learn DIY and mechanics even though I had few skills but my father-in-law Barry has been the most perfect reference book, guide and surrogate father having been a very practical man all his life and my mother-in-law Linda, I have been blessed with quite frankly. She's made things so easy and has always been there at the drop of a hat. In fact it was a bit of a family joke that if I was to even mention a project I intended to do with the house or a repair to my car she would automatically say, "Oh, Barry will do that for you, won't you Barry?"

Becky and I would turn up at their house and poor Barry's dinner was divided up and added to, to provide food for all of us, and she insisted I drink his beer too. So for 20 years, I would do everything to save labour costs on the house or car, my car never went to the garage for 20 years apart from for its MOT. Barry gave constant advice, diagrams and encouragement which gave me the specific skills and confidence to dive in and give it a go. He would then sort me out if I got completely tied up or if it were beyond my skill. He could turn his hand to anything and I've been incredibly lucky to have someone like that to learn so much from.

Things almost didn't work out when I first started going out with Becky. My first date was not an official one but consisted of me going out with her big brother and their lifelong male friends as well. It seemed I passed the test until I walked her back from my singles quarters at 3am in the morning, kissing her goodnight at the door after a rather romantic evening shall we

113

say. She was temporarily living above the chip shop and as she backed away through the glass door I noticed the outline of her Dad, a huge imposing and stern figure with his arms crossed and standing absolutely still. I wanted to warn Becky but I just had to watch her back away into the gloom.

As I walked back up the hill towards my singles quarters, my mind was racing two to the dozen. Barry was quite a strict Dad I thought, but whereas a couple of boyfriends had fallen foul in the past, I wasn't going to make the same mistake. I needed him on side. He would insist the bedroom door was left open when we were in there and although she was 18, he insisted on a curfew for her too which I had well and truly broken with her. I wondered what my Dad would have done as he was a gent but he would have just as easily got into a similar scrape, no doubt, so as I wondered what he may have done in this situation I had an idea.

The following afternoon I was due to see Becky again at her parents' cafe. I opened the glass door and met Becky who told me her Dad was not pleased with me at all. I ascended the narrow stairs to the flat avoiding the snapping jaws of their Jack Russell named Snoopy as I did so, and entered the lounge area where I could see Barry leaning with his hands behind him, leaning back against the wall rocking gently to and fro. He looked at me as I approached him and his stern expression didn't change. I said, "Sorry Mr Harding, the party went on a bit long last night, I do hope you'll accept this token as an apology. We should have let you know".

I could hear my late father saying the words as I mouthed them. He had a way with words. In my outstretched hand was a bottle of Gordon's Gin which I already knew he liked. He gently took hold of the bottle and wandered towards the kitchen, and with a relaxed soft voice said, "Will you have one with me?"

Becky was staring in disbelief at the whole episode and I remember distinctly the words she mouthed, "He's never done that before!"

As I have been married to Becky for 26 years now, I am very close to Barry now and I confess I have teased him several times reminding him I technically bought his daughter for a bottle of gin! A small dowry!

We now live in a house where my hands have touched every centimetre and probably several times over with DIY projects. New floors, rendering the walls, new ceilings, wiring, plumbing, kitchens, bathrooms, and then there's the cars over the years, the gearboxes, replacing engines, new head gaskets and I remember having my Mazda 626 engine block in my kitchen with every part of the head in pieces. "Becky?" I asked in a nervous voice. She walked in to see a thousand widgets and grommets neatly labelled on my kitchen table. The sight slightly unnerved her as she had seen that under the bonnet of the car was now distinctly lacking many engine parts! They were now all on my kitchen table! "Becky, I have no idea how all this goes back".

Now instead of freaking out, she replied, "Okay love, let's just think. Just give it a go and see how you get on, you'll be okay".

I loved her for that and quickly put her mind at rest telling her, "Na love, I'll have it together in a few hours!"

It showed me what she would be like in a small crisis. This was our only car and there was the possibility that instead of fixing it over a weekend and saving a valuable £300, I could have in fact destroyed a car worth £800. I love her for her calm attitude and her utter support as she has shown me numerous times in our 26 years of marriage.

When I phoned her from halfway through my basic Initial Firearms Course having realised I just couldn't hit a barn door with a 9mm bullet at that time, she was the same calm sensible practical support to me. I clearly remember the time when I failed an Operational Firearms Commanders course, Team Leader to you and me, I was standing in the same kitchen I rebuilt my Mazda engine in, she could see the utter devastation on my face but she spoke calmly and softly, lightening a path of hope I knew that given a short time of self-pity I could soon begin to walk down again.

I tell the young police officers on my section now when they are scraping around for money and wondering how they are going to continue doing the shifts, getting the kids to school whilst their wives also work and they have the stress of the huge mortgage to pay, I tell them of the time many years previously when I thought the same, listening to a Radio 2 money expert guest. After that interview I clearly remember thinking, "Well there it is, I'm never going to own a house. There isn't enough land, the costs are huge and I just am not ever going to be able to afford one". But without any financial help at all, no money left to me through wills whatsoever or given to us or Rebecca we now have our own house we can soon pay off. Doing all the mechanics all those years ago and still doing my DIY has saved us enormous amounts of cash. Rebecca and I have had our own private limited company importing Artificial Topiary Balls, random I know, which has speeded things along a bit by creating more savings for us but it's been hard work. We never borrowed money, a concept I couldn't understand back then either, but seems to be so natural nowadays.

I am extremely fortunate to have my wife, children and my Border Terrier Jack Russell cross called Arthur who has often saved my sanity in times of stress. My dog is my life I have to say and I always get into trouble when we have the "order of love" conversation! Okay, I do like to wind them up a little!

13. The Dark

I have suffered from night terrors for many years now and I have finally given up trying to subdue them. I should more accurately say my wife suffers from them as often in the morning I cheerfully ask, "Morning love, sleep well?" The scowl I receive tells me what's coming next, "Oh very well Harry, apart from the five occasions you had me up pulling you back into bed, with you screaming 'we are all going to die!'"

Ah, well I would often put up a defence of her being a very light sleeper but this never washed. Sometimes I hadn't a clue I had woken during the night but often, usually when approaching a course I had to complete or there was something on my mind I would get a night terror or three and usually remember each one of them. It was usually about half an hour into my sleep when rapid eye movement (REM) occurred. It's the period when you fall into the deepest and most rewarding sleep or supposedly of course!

This would often mean me suddenly shouting and running around the room in total darkness. I realised very quickly I was "problem solving" of sorts, in other words I would find myself in the back of a van loading it and knowing there were some random children or a family in the cab at the front and it starts to roll away down a steep hill. The van is going too fast for me to jump out and I cannot get to the cab to put the brakes on. The van is gaining momentum, bouncing around and I am hanging on for dear life. If you imagine this for real, I mean really as if it were real you have the very same sensation of movement, the same adrenaline rush, the same fear and sense of impending doom and then you are halfway there to knowing how it feels.

Those children are all going to die... and it's all my fault. They are going to die and there is nothing I can do to change it... and I await the impact when BANG, I wake with a jolt or with Rebecca desperately trying to hold on to me to stop me climbing out of the bed and inevitably injuring myself. My heart is racing at 180 beats per minute and it's bouncing out of my chest. I feel my recently diagnosed but believed harmless heart murmur is being tested to the nth degree. I slump back into bed and much to my exhausted wife's annoyance, I'm asleep in 2 minutes, my wife taking a considerable time longer to do the same.

I was receiving a number of injuries such as pulled muscles by pulling vehicles off the trapped victims in my dream, or what was in fact my double bed with Rebecca still in it, poor girl. I realised my injuries I collected were taking longer than usual to repair and I even recently pulled the wardrobe door off! There I was awake wondering what the hell I was walking around the bedroom with a mirrored door in my hands. Fortunately I fixed it so it opens the other side now so problem solved for now! In fact I realised how to fix it before I had even got back to sleep! You just can't shake those minor injuries off anymore however and they hang around for months which seems to be the main problem I have at the moment.

I decided I would go to my GP who advised me to go to a clinic to see if there was anything they could do to help me. He did tell me not to be alarmed with the name of the clinic as they also dealt with issues other than mine. It was called the Anxiety and Depression Clinic. I just wanted to know if there was a switch I could turn to get rid of these things, just to save my wife's sanity if anything. I know readers are screaming for Rebecca to get a spare room but with two 20 years olds using the other two rooms, that's tricky.

I turn up at the Anxiety and Depression Clinic; this is before everyone had Anxiety and Depression, before it became a badge of honour to many. I can see some readers slamming this book shut in disgust if they have managed to drag themselves through it thus far, "How could I be so disrespectful?" Well, I am completely empathetic to those who have it and are trying to battle these genuinely awful afflictions and I thank my atheist God every day I don't suffer from the same but I am not being contradictory, I promise you. I have however, seen many from my experiences in my job who throw it up like a badge of honour which is supposed to excuse their criminal behaviour.

I don't like the way no one can challenge now. In the police we understand some of the more dubious public can lie to get an advantage in life, and although I don't go so far as to say many lie, if they are diagnosed with a very difficult to diagnose affliction it means they can if they choose, withdraw from everyday life. Many who may be misdiagnosed may feel they are doomed for life and therefore it's not worth trying to better themselves. I was recently at a flat speaking with four teenage witnesses to a public order outside their flat. They were secure inside but one called the police because a small 19 year old girl had been banging their front door with her fists. I was filling in the usual requirements to not only assist with their safeguarding process, but also to collect statistics which no one believes anyway but the government puts so much on! So I have to ask these 21st century routine questions, 'Do you consider yourself vulnerable?" Within a beat, the reply came back one by one as "Yes".

"Okay", I reply slightly bemused, "in which way do you feel you are vulnerable?"

"I have anxiety and depression".

All four of them replied one by one. When a few years ago you would be a bit down and a little worried or anxious about something, now it's automatic to say you are suffering from anxiety and depression. I see these young people withdrawing from any responsibilities, they don't go for jobs, can't get jobs, and "can't be bothered as I'm on disability". Then I see those that are suffering from extreme anxiety and depression. Those you realise desperately need the help but can't get it because the system is overloaded with the not so anxious and depressed but who are actually naturally worried and sad, but someone turned those natural feelings into a medical condition, all in the name of political correctness. Those that need it are ignored and those that shout the loudest get the badge. There are those that say they don't have the energy to get up in the morning but miraculously find it late at night when they cause the police to be called out every five minutes and I know this because I know if I went to the doctor and said, "I don't sleep, I get stressed sometimes, I get migraines, I don't want to get up in the morning sometimes, I am tired most of the time, and I've been to horrible scenes", all things that are true from time to time, what diagnosis do you think they would give me? If anyone was to challenge this, they are verbally beaten down. I don't blame the doctors too much either because all those symptoms I have said could well mean I could be depressed and suffering from anxiety at another time. The political correctness of not questioning the overuse of this term means those that need help probably won't get it. Those that have been diagnosed with it who maybe shouldn't have, feel their lives are over. They have been given a label they will now struggle to get over. 'I can't get a job because I suffer from anxiety and depression.' Game over.

I turn up in the waiting room. Sit down and wait as the term implies but I am soon called into a small office with a comfortable woman in a cardigan and baggy trousers. She has frizzy grey hair and she is looking sideways over her spectacles towards me. Okay, I must be talking to an art teacher but here goes.

"Before we start, can you fill this form in please?" she asks. "Circle the numbers that best fit how you feel. 1 is not at all well, and 10 is you feel very bad."

The first question is easy, so is the second and the third. 1, 1, and 1. And so it continues... "Do you feel suicidal? How much do you feel depressed? Do you find it difficult to get out of bed?"

The art teacher intervenes... "Er, Mr Tangye, the '1' is that you don't feel bad at all?" I can tell she must be thinking I have completely mixed up the scoring process because otherwise, why would I be there?

"Yes", I replied, "I know it seems strange but I will explain". I was sure I was in the wrong place but hell I've got nothing to lose, right? So then we have a chat, not about art but about my night terrors and after a discussion of my problem-solving at work, problem-solving at home with my small business and DIY etc, I found I was getting no break time. My brain, as small as it was, was not getting any rest. I should take the dog out more, I should get away from things a bit, I should learn to relax, oh and it's called Parasomnia. I was quietly pleased, it was a cool name. No one wanted a stupid named affliction such as lazy-omna, or weak-omnia. I was cool with it… after all I didn't dread going to sleep, I could see how some would fear it but I didn't. I was very fortunate indeed but I just needed to regularly repair bedroom furniture and recover from strained muscles over longer periods of time as I got older.

Rebecca would often say it was no surprise after what I had seen over nearly 30 years in front-line policing attending hundreds of serious and fatal road traffic collisions. Working in Armed Response in Devon and Cornwall we had a lesser crime rate than other forces and yet we were huge geographically speaking so it made sense we were dual-rolled with the Traffic Department or more accurately attending serious and fatal road traffic collisions. I was a Senior Investigating Officer for 15 years and I still attend and scene-manage fatals up to the end of my service.

To be frank, I have been very fortunate and I am quite sure it doesn't have anything to do with the scenes I've attended. I've seen an awful lot of dead people, often in a disfigured or mutilated state. I manage to section this all off. Dead is dead; I live for the living. I am a soppy git when it comes to that and I often shed a discrete tear when dealing with humanity. Any emotional tale on television can get me going. Just a tear, nothing too obvious but maybe it is to others who choose to save my blushes. I wonder if this is a pressure release that has saved me for so long stopping me from going mad. I don't get flashbacks of grizzly sights, I block these out completely, but I have strange memories of all those fatalities.

I talked about Anna Norrish for a road safety campaign called Learn2Live. I was involved in this campaign aimed at students for over 10 years. Anna was killed when she was a passenger in a car whose driver she didn't know had been drinking. When remembering this account early on I couldn't remember her face and when I was asked to speak to her mother some time later I had to pull my statement to remind myself of the details of the scene.

I remembered her bare feet and flip flops in the footwell of the car as this memory was completely out of context. Those bare feet and flip flops should have been on a beach but they were in this deadly collision scene instead. For some reason this is the picture in my mind I tend to remember and the gruesome stuff tends to be locked up away from my visual memory. If those lockers are ever opened one day then maybe I will struggle a bit. Anna's mother Ali, I now know very well and consider to be a good friend as she also talked at the road safety campaign too. It's all about empowering students to take control of a dangerous situation in a car if they are a passenger, considering that most fatalities occur in the front passenger seat. We call it the sacrificial seat. We try to empower them by telling the driver to either slow down, or they feel sick which will probably have the same effect or if they see the driver is getting tired over a long drive, to give them ideas such as telling the driver they want a coffee or they need the loo at the next services. Ali has done incredible work to use the devastating loss of her beautiful daughter to get this message across.

I do however remember one particular scene. I don't know why it pops up in my memory now having lain dormant for so long and now and then just giving me the odd poke in the ribs to say hello. Someone had driven their car without a seatbelt on, and certainly not at any speed. They had got a right-hand bend wrong and the car had climbed a metal Armco which gently rolled the car over onto its roof. Unfortunately as the driver had not been wearing a seatbelt he half rolled out of the open window and the torso and head were caught under the roof with the feet caught in the pedals of the car. The car used the extra bodily fluid lubrication to slide along the road leaving a meter wide trail of blood and debris in its wake. It wasn't pleasant and we knew what was in store for us when the car was rolled back onto its wheels.

It was sometime before we were ready to right the car again and it was one of the few times I had a word with myself beforehand. This was going to be grizzly. The car rolled back over gently revealing the scream mask. No structure to the skull, just a bag and an 'O' expression I will never forget. That one can be a little cheeky sometimes but generally it tends to leave me alone.

14. Childbirth and Promotion

Promotion was something I had never intended to get into. It wasn't for me. I often felt I was blagging it as a PC quite frankly. One day someone would find out I was a fraud and the game would be up. I didn't have A levels, I had some ropey O'levels and CSE's and this got me through the process because all that was required was 'about 5 O'levels' and I scraped them along with a separate maths and English test on application.

This is why I now feel so angry there is a huge move just as big business is moving away from degrees and getting into apprenticeships instead, the police seem to be doing the opposite. The College of Policing does some great work ensuring a national approach to policing as I know the training set for Armed Response is universal so whatever training they get in West Mids, Manchester and the Met, I get too. This drive for degrees to be a police officer is so damaging for our future of policing; I would not have stood a chance if I were to join now, I would not have met the level required. The College of Policing will insist that officers can join with no degree still. The equivalent of an A level or level 3 qualification is still required which would still have counted me out from applying. It certainly sounds good if you have achieved that, as a new recruit will be paid between an £18,000 and £23,000 salary to complete a policing degree and their training. The other alternative would be to do it independently at their own cost and have a shorter course on entry but who would do that?

How wonderful for intellectually clever students though. Instead of having a percentage of their wage removed to pay off a large student loan, they get paid a reasonable salary instead. Notice this suits only inexperienced young people. What are those so vitally needed experienced ex-military going to do? What about those people who have been in the work stream for 10 years already and have a family to support, a mortgage to pay? And what is this degree going to achieve? When leaving the Force do they think an employer is going to ask, "So you have one of these generic policing degrees do you?" Or are they going to ask, "So what did you do in the police?" The degree will count for little, and will attract many student academics and few others.

We need officers with degrees, we really do but we need a spread of society in the police. We need those practical enough to put a decent file together but it's more important to have someone who can think on their feet, can have integrity, those that care for the community, those that don't mind getting cold and wet occasionally, and prepared to face an angry crowd. If those that enter all want to achieve promotion they will soon get disillusioned. All that talent wasted who could have done so much good in the police are now not qualified to even apply for the police or perhaps didn't think they could achieve the degree result so relied upon.

If I were a cynic, I would say the only reason this has been brought about is because the government is offering an apprenticeship levy. Money is paid by the government to train students to degree level. What will happen when this ends? Well, they will insist the officer already has a degree no doubt, a bit like in nursing. A tragedy where some nurses who didn't want to specialise could have been the most wonderful hard-working carers who learned so much on the job, and this now perhaps accounts for the massive shortfall of nurse numbers, about 40,000 at the moment and I don't see why policing should be any different in the future once the options start reducing for recruits. Degrees are a necessity for certain areas and will help in other areas, but for a person who wants to do their bit for the community it's a disgrace they won't be able to if they can't afford the pay drop or they don't wish to undertake a totally unnecessary degree which probably won't count for much anyway.

So fortunately I got in before all this nonsense as I wouldn't have had the capability or the inclination of completing this at the time. I just wanted to know how I could get out there and find the bad guys and help the good guys. It's very important to me to maintain the respect of the police to the public. I did not join the police to be insulted or abused, which unfortunately more and more officers feel is part of the job; taking verbal abuse from some piece of slime who contributes nothing to society and takes everything from it was certainly not for me. If you let abuse just happen or wash over you then the next police officer is going to get it twice as bad. The respect for the post of officer has left the criminal and antisocial yob, and society suffers as a result. Society has a lot to answer for however because it's permitted the media and politicians to allow the criminal to have the upper hand. It gives them all the rights and ensures it picks holes in the police officers' behaviour no matter what the provocation or even criticising their tactics when offering no other solution. To be completely honest with you I never found the need to swear using the F word towards a member of the public. I felt that was putting myself below them but, my, I could give them a bollocking they'd never had before. A double barrelled verbal shotgun straight between the eyes but that did come with confidence and practice.

My Section always knew I was losing my patience with some drunken idiot involving himself in scraps in the high street when my voice became posher in tone! It was quite common for some 21 year old to insist he knew more about the law than I did and that I had no right to move him on. Having directed him to google Section 3 of the Criminal Law Act whilst shoving him down the high street I'd then inform him "a little knowledge is dangerous" and to "run along now".

The alcohol in his system would inevitably encourage much Dutch courage, and he'd come back like a petulant child insisting on his protest so I would waft him away with my hand whilst looking in the other direction dismissively saying, "Are you still here? You are boring me now, go away or I will have to arrest you". It may even come to calling his bluff and simulating a radio transmission requesting a riot van to take him away which would normally work if he hadn't taken the hint.

What should have happened of course is to give these oiks a lesson in the first place and to lock them up but that means taking two officers off the street for 4 hours at least, and that's before you even calculate the other officer hours used in the morning for interviewing and file preparation. It's something I can talk about a little more freely now, but it's important people realise there are not 20 officers dealing with a city's crime. There are often as few as 6 to 8 officers answering all the calls in a city the size of Exeter or in an area the size of Torbay. Out of those 8, you can guarantee 2 officers will have been taken up for most of the shift with a mental health incident as there simply isn't the investment in mental health services to take it off the police hands, and 2 officers would soon end up in hospital waiting with a prisoner who is pretending he's knocked his head or swallowed some drugs, just so he gets better surroundings other than a police cell and has the pleasure of inconveniencing 2 other police officers. Society has basically been taken for total mugs by these repeat offenders and the lawyers mean there is nothing we can do to rectify it.

Before we go on, I'll quickly explain the injustices of why suspects are treated with kid gloves in custody when it's clear the officers are being taken advantage of and why this means there are fewer officers to deal with preventing and detecting crime.

I certainly can't blame the custody Sergeants for insisting these detainees be taken to hospital and then who often have to wait with the rest of the public in triage, especially as any death in custody can destroy a police officer's career, heart and soul and often where he was merely doing his job.

I have a very good colleague who is a shadow of his former self but recovering slowly who had been destroyed by the system when an extremely violent male with mental health issues stopped breathing in the cells. CCTV clearly showed he was treated with extreme care but there was of course criticism that the man should have been monitored more often than he had been; we are talking minutes here, not hours. For the next 6 years my colleague thought he may be going to prison and went through 2 manslaughter Crown Court cases before being found not guilty along with several other detention officers who had been on duty at the time. His words to me say it all, "Harry, I still don't know what I was supposed to have done wrong. No one has told me yet". How you treat a human this way I have no idea. It's quite frankly unjust and completely disgusting and is currently a "There for the grace of God" situation whether you pick up the rod as an officer or someone else does before you. Whether it's your time or someone else's and that just isn't right.

Of course the public hear the one version in incidents such as this, rightly so they hear a lot from the grieving family who will often say how terrible the police have been and of course they want to blame everyone apart from themselves. The police are not able to answer as the investigation rumbles on for years on end. It's that drip, drip of one sided character assassination slowly corroding the officer's brain and soul. He's suspended from his normal duties, colleagues don't know what to say to him, he just festers for years on end until finally he is cleared, the family cry foul, and all is forgotten except for the utter devastation left in the investigation's wake.

I have found the complaints system is completely led by those that shout loudest and of course the police are not permitted to shout loudly. We have to remain quiet until after the case. We have to listen to the drivel piped out by the families on how awful the police were and how they are covering things up. Let me tell you, the custody suit is the place where service is better than most hotels as the staff are paranoid of having a death or injury at their hands. Annual custody death statistics are piped out by campaigners with agendas with the huge assumption the deaths were due to the police. If you were to stand in a custody suit and see the violent, suicidal and mentally ill flowing through during the night, you would be staggered that the deaths were so few across the whole country. Unfortunately society should admit that it's inevitable there will be deaths from time to time when dealing with the most dangerous and psychotic people in society and sometimes it just isn't anybody's fault when one commits suicide in a cell and isn't got to in time. It's just a tragic event overall where the whole of society has failed, and should not scapegoat the police.

The IOPC listen to the family baying for police blood, threatening riots in London and the authorities listen to them mainly for political or financial grounds. The authorities have to appear humble and they don't want to spend huge amounts of much needed money dealing with riots. It should be suggesting to these families that perhaps if their guidance had been better as parents, then their budding musician or footballer son may not have swallowed the drugs when being stop searched and choked himself. Perhaps the parents should realise when they washed their hands of their child they shouldn't expect the police to accept responsibility for their own failings instead. Okay, I'm spouting on now. I hate injustice though, and these officers who have been suspended from their everyday work have their lives put on hold for years. It's worse than that because they cannot apply for promotion, they cannot move department, and they often have to shuffle paper around an office for years. It's not what they joined for. It's disgusting and I feel that one day there will be a national outcry where all these poor souls will be due huge amounts of compensation because their own human rights were thrown to the wall. What is clear is any officer being investigated is treating a hundred times worse than a criminal, even when there is no immediate evidence of wrongdoing. It's wrong, wrong, wrong.

As a single-crewed PC on the Traffic Department I saw a black male driving his car and he wasn't wearing his seat belt. I will be honest, I did hesitate as I felt it would be easier to ignore this situation but I then felt my integrity would not be up to scratch if I was to prosecute white people but not a black person for the same offence. Should I only deal with white offenders? Was I being racist to presume this person would act in any other way by making a false complaint against me compared to any other driver I stopped? I pulled the car over and informed him politely I had stopped him as he was not wearing a seat belt. I offered him the choice for it to be heard in court but I was prepared to deal with it by means of a ticket. I had said these words a hundred times before with other motorists. I had already dealt with many RTC's where the driver or passenger hadn't been wearing a seatbelt and had been badly injured. Their carelessness was now going to cost the taxpayer an awful lot of unnecessary and much needed cash to keep them in intensive care as opposed to being an outpatient in A&E. This is indeed if the collision hadn't killed them of course.

He refused to give me his name and address and whatever amount of gentle requests and cajoling, whatever amount of "You will leave me with no other alternative" pleas by myself I had the ridiculously unnecessary requirement but to arrest him in order to establish details fit for the service of a summons. I treated him as a gentleman, and apart from the being awkward for the sake of it, he was relatively pleasant to deal with. I took him to custody and on arrival he gave his details and I returned him to his car. Some days later I found out he had made a complaint against me stating I'd been racially abusive towards him. I was devastated at first, but then angry, and when it eventually came to me being interviewed by my Force Professional Standards Unit, I walked into the room where the tapes were all set up with a positive attitude, or maybe I was just a little bit angry.

The tapes were switched on, (yes, they were tapes then), and the Superintendent interviewer leaned forward to ask his first question, but I interjected. "Excuse me, Sir, I'd like to give a quick statement".

He looked a little shocked. "Er, yes, by all means".

"I want to make it known on the tape I am angry. I am angry that I treated this man as a gentleman with all the respect anyone should. There was no argument, no aggression, no shouting, but he has used his colour to not only try to get himself out of a ticket, he has used it to try to get me sacked which would lead to huge stresses for myself and my family, the loss of my house and pressure on my family. I am angry but I refuse to let this man lose me any sleep, I won't give him the pleasure. I despise him right now for what he has done, so please don't take my answers as being arrogant. You won't have any evidence, if I had been racist towards him I would be cacking it right now, thinking maybe you had a recording he'd secretly taken, but you won't have one as there was no racism; so ask your questions, I will answer and then I will walk out of here and get on with my life".

After a momentary stunned silence, and after a very short interview, the interviewer asked me a question which changed my life. "PC Tangye, have you ever thought of going for promotion?"

No I hadn't but it made me think. He'd obviously been impressed with the way I'd held myself, my integrity and sense of duty, but honesty as well. I had 3 weeks left to order the revision books and to register before the deadline for that year. I passed the exam first time around and also the part two Osprey practical stations assessments a year after that. I was on a charge. I only had a local interview to go and I was put forward with an 'Outstanding' Recommend. Now at this time my wife was very pregnant with twins, a boy and a girl. Job done all at once, just perfect. Three weeks before the due date, Rebecca's waters broke at 4am and I drove her to the hospital. My interview before the panel for promotion to Sergeant was to be on the following day.

14 hours later and 6lb 1oz Rowan popped out without too much trouble. Well I would say that I guess, I suspect you may receive a slightly different version from my wife. Whilst now holding Rowan in my arms, it was Savannah's turn just 10 minutes later. There was a problem. She was breach and her arm was twisted and caught. I remember looking at her legs and bottom fully exposed, but she was caught and they couldn't release her. The midwife or consultant by this time I wouldn't be able to say, were twisting her around using every method available to release her and I was transfixed in terror for several heart stopping seconds before suddenly she's out. Her arm, very floppy and I'm waiting for the first breath and cry just as I did with Rowan, but nothing. Just silence except for the scurrying around from all the staff.

Being a copper, I have often seen other emergency services about their work and I know very clearly when things aren't going well for them. I could see the sense of urgency on their faces. The life of my daughter was completely in their hands. There was nothing I could do. I asked, "Is she going to be alright?"

The answer was not one of comfort: "We are doing all we can".

It dawned on me, something I had never even considered. Were we going to be taking just one baby home? Home to a bedroom with two prams, two cots, and two sets of baby clothes. Would we be attending a funeral and a christening? I was scared, very scared.

And then out of the blue the cry of a baby. Savannah had entered the world with the full intention of receiving as much attention as she possibly could. Her performance was complete. We could relax, although she did look like a Tesco chicken at 4lb 10.

I left my wife Rebecca to recover in hospital after we had eaten fish and chips her parents had brought with them. She was exhausted bless her, she had gone through hell but we were now a family and it felt good.

Strangely enough, I attended my promotion interview the following day and flunked it! I didn't care that much because I now had a family so I had other things on my mind. I did wonder however if I had been the only candidate in history who'd managed to fail his interview with an 'Outstanding' Recommend! I'm sort of proud of that!

The happy ending here is that one year later I attended another interview and got through. I was now a Sergeant and now it only had to be decided by the bosses where I would be posted.

Back then Sir John Evans was the Chief Constable, a formidable and thoroughly feared but well respected boss. I was well settled in Armed Response and I knew that once I had left on promotion I may never get back to it again. I was desperate to stay put. I called Personnel and schmoozed them as much as I could.

The answer was final... I will leave firearms for extra experience and I would have to reapply and possibly have to requalify from scratch at a later date.

The date was set for the meeting with the Chief and the other 12 successful candidates to decide our fate. In the meantime my schmoozing continued with Personnel as I was desperate to work in Torbay. I had completed 5 years there already including 2 years probation and I had returned after 3 years of working in Dawlish, a beautiful seaside town between Torbay and Exeter. Torbay also meant I would be able to cycle into work but the environment wasn't such a hot topic back then, we were still busily destroying it so I knew there was only a chance I would get my wish.

The date arrived and I nervously queued up with the other candidates. We all discussed our preferences amongst ourselves and filed into the large conference room with a huge central table. There were no windows in this central command, designed against terrorist attack, so I'm told. There was a large screen at the end with a significantly larger chair with armrests dictating it was the boss's position.

We were sitting around the table with a large piece of A4 paper in front of us. We had also discussed amongst ourselves the poor naive individuals who had informed the Chief the location they were designated to work in was not conducive to them. "Yes Sir, if it's okay to wait for a position nearer to home, I'd very much appreciate that".

"Yes officer, I'm sure that won't be a problem". Needless to say, they were rarely offered another position so the rumours went.

The door opens and we all stand bolt upright in our immaculate tunics, looking towards the door at the silhouette of the Chief entering, standing in the doorway, and then he slowly walked into the room. Was that a white cat he was stroking? No, it was my imagination but everything else was set for him to be the Bond villain.

"Good morning gentlemen". Yes, I was right, Bond villain.

"Good morning, Sir", we all say in unison. I suppressed the urge to continue with "Good morning everyone" taking myself back to my primary school greeting when the teacher came into the room.

Sir John then proceeded with a short speech outlining what he expected. He insisted on us coming in to work half an hour before the shift to prepare the briefing etc. Something I have always done ever since. We knew he would check, too. And then the finale, "Well Gentlemen, you can turn over your papers, see your designated stations you will be stationed at." I paused as others quickly spun their papers over revealing the stations. There were many satisfying gasps. I put my hand on my paper, and before I could turn it over Sir John said, "Are we all happy, Gentlemen?"

"Yes Sir... very happy", I replied without even turning it over. I was not going to be that naive officer. Get promoted first, worry about it later but you never know, surely it will be Torbay. I turned the paper over and saw the word 'Plymouth'. Face drained, busy, busy city, 88 mile round trip, no parking, hellish!

"Perfect, Sir, thank you", I repeated.

I motorbiked it to Plymouth for the next 3 years. Only fell asleep on it twice, I think. Getting home with a dent in the top of the fuel tank where the helmet has hit it... okay I exaggerate a little but I did spend three very happy years in Plymouth, the most wonderful of proving grounds. If you can Sergeant in Plymouth Response you should be able to do it anywhere in the Force. Even though I tried all I could to stay in Firearms at Exeter or to go to Torbay where I lived, it was the best thing that could have happened to me for that period of time and I was fortunately able to return to Firearms afterwards; and just to highlight some of the fun experiences I had whilst working as a Response Sergeant in Plymouth, I need to mention the following.

Union Street in Plymouth was an infamous street many Navy personnel will remember fondly. It was a nightclub strip all the sailors used to use and often it was the first stop when they found some leave. Policing it was, well, interesting. There were regularly drunken fights and skirmishes breaking out mainly from the civilian locals. We would spread ourselves along the strip and I had 3 transit van loads of Police personnel at my hands. The night sometimes would drag especially if it was cold so we used to try to do things up to spice it up a little and make time go quicker.

One night I made it a task for officers to get as many "Top Gun" quotes in on the radio as they could. The competition was on. The "You can be my wingman" comment was the first when one officer helped another with an arrest which had been particularly problematic. The drunk man who had used his 'All you can drink for £20' ticket to full effect created quite an unnecessarily aggressive struggle with some officers, the chap was unceremoniously handcuffed and shoved into the cell at the rear of the van, a little like folding a particularly long tentacled octopus into a small wardrobe. The chap still not having had his fill of picking on an innocent passer-by or fighting with police and being thrown into custody, decides in his wisdom it would improve his cause no end if he was to repeatedly smash his head against the side of the van. The stage was set and the arresting officer quipped to his crew mate, "I feel the need... "

"...the need for speed" returned the officer getting into the passenger side.

"It needs to be on the radio!" I shouted as they drove off. The van disappeared with the prisoner towards custody and things began to die down a bit.

About an hour later from out of the blue... the radio came into life, "Tower this is Ghost Rider, requesting a flyby".

The van was on its way back and I realised it was my line now. "Negative Ghost Rider, the pattern is full".

I can only imagine the faces in the control room who were not aware of the shenanigans but no doubt were slowly getting the idea.

The Police van approached at speed and instead of pulling up where it should, it buzzed by me quite closely causing me to step back! "God Damned!" I shouted, "Get me another coffee!"

I was in the lead van of the three returning back to base at 3am. Everyone was tired and looking forward to clocking off when one of the girls said those famous Top Gun words on the radio. "Take me to bed or lose me forever!"

The cheers from the vans were loud enough to cover any reply and no doubt any shock from the radio operator. The night was complete.

15. A Debt Repaid

Double-crewed with John, we are patrolling the area in and around Exeter and it's a winter's evening, pitch black but otherwise a pleasant evening. The call comes in from the Force Incident Manager, (FIM): "You are authorised for firearms, chaps, getting a call of a teenager running around with a gun, believed black pistol, recognised by an ex-military member of public". He was concerned enough to call it in and it seems the owner of the gun wasn't being too careful about hiding from view.

I am already winding the car up putting the blue lights on to help clear a path through the city. They'll come off as we get nearer and it isn't long before we are near the scene, so silent approach on this. The update is he's about 25, white European, slim build in a dark coat and blue jeans. He's been showing the gun to other males he seems to know. It's near Exeter City Football Club and he was last seen walking into South View Terrace. It's now 10pm and there are also some drinkers about. We are updated on the male's demeanour, believed skittish and unpredictable but let's keep this in context... could be something or nothing. The next is fast. We have Glock pistols in holsters, and we see a possible suspect in the shadows. It's a low level threat as there have been no other calls, but we have to remain sharp.

We've abandoned our car and are slowly making are way on foot towards him on the other side of the road about 20 metres away. There are no other firearms units nearby at this time; we could lose him if we wait so I decide to get out on foot with John to support him. I cannot handle a gun and a car at the same time and we are satisfied it's still relatively low threat. Exeter is not Manchester, but we cannot be blasé. We have drugs problems in our cities, towns and villages, just like everyone else. We are fortunate we don't have the level of gun crime as others may do, but nevertheless we do meet some nasty sods who like to pay us a visit now and then to get a bit of the action, drugs action.

A bit of a pincer movement on him as we approach but he glances up, no gun in hand, good, but he's off. He's got a guilty conscience so it seems we have the right person. We obviously won't shoot someone who hasn't got a weapon in his hands so John is after him with me on his heels. John is challenging him, Glock pistols now in our hands. He shouts, "Stop, armed police!"

The youth spins around and grabs something within his jacket throwing it on the floor. It's a gun. "It's only a BB Gun" he shouts, but he's feeling brave, ignoring John's demands for him to get on the floor. After a momentary standoff delay I see my chance and grab the guy by the jacket, swinging him around so the momentum carries him onto the ground. He's all legs and arms and squeals in pain. "You, Sir, are nicked", I shout in his ear. I look at John expecting to see the face of victory, but he's not happy. Not happy at all.

The gun was a BB gun, we are always disappointed about that, but our official response is we are glad of course! Having booked the lad into custody for being in possession of a firearm or imitation firearm with intent to cause fear of violence we completed the necessary paperwork. John was still stony-faced. "Come on, John" I said. I had broken and wanted to know what the problem was. I was not going to wait any longer. "You nicked my arrest, Harry. He was mine, but that's okay, no problems, but he was mine and you just came in and took it".

Now arrests used to be very competitive in the old days. When I say that, I mean when there were far more officers, when the paperwork didn't include a tonne of safeguarding and statistic collecting, all incredibly necessary to someone no doubt but it meant that making arrests wasn't so much fun anymore. Don't get me wrong, they had to be good arrests to count. Certain public order offences didn't count because everyone had different thresholds. You could rush out to a job, arrest someone and within 2 hours you were on the street again. To attend a job today, fill out the paperwork at the scene and then in custody can take all day to complete. One job and you're done. More often than not now, you can get a handful of officers at an incident looking at a crumpled heap of snot on the ground hoping someone else is going to make the arrest before them.

I thought this was a one-off with John and we'd soon be back to normal, but John mentioned this several times during the following week as well. It didn't look like he was going to let it go. We'd have a mug of tea for briefing and he'd say, "Harry mate, this one's mine okay, don't want you nicking it". It was friendly banter but there was clearly a huge annoyance behind it. Had I? Had I nicked the arrest off him? I had hands on first. Our arrest league tables were pretty close. I cannot remember who was ahead so I will say it was me for the purposes of the book!

It came to the point when we were in the kitchen with the rest of the Section having a cup of tea. It was John's turn to drive and he took the keys. "That's if you aren't going to take them first, Harry".

I suddenly sprung up from my seat flinging my chair back. John reacted in a defensive mode, pushing himself away from the table looking startled. His reaction startled me which startled him. It was all very startling!

I gently removed a 4 inch plastic silver trophy cup from my pocket. I had been waiting for this moment and hadn't needed to wait very long.

I pronounced to the whole room with great gusto, "It is with great pride, I now present John with this Trophy for being winger of the week!"

The applause was immediate by all. John gracefully accepted the fully engraved Trophy at some considerable time and expense by me, well okay; I had stolen my child's old swimming trophy from home and scribbled the words on a ripped piece of paper, stuck on with sticky tape. No effort and no expense, but it broke the ice and I don't think my daughter has noticed even today her beloved 25m swimming race trophy disappeared from the bottom draw. I know; bad parent.

But that isn't the end.

Me at 11 years old.
Newquay Tretherras
School. Cracking hair cut!

In 1988, there was no prouder
Mum. Special Constable 532.

Dawlish 1994. Showing
off the latest Police
Ford Escort Panda Car

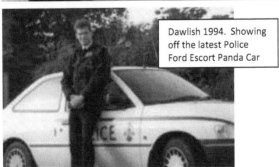

March 2015. This
started everything
when the Mail
Online entitled my
tweet, "Traffic Cop's
Bizarre Selfie".
Twitter then took
off

I was asked if I could assist in a quick photo (on passenger
side). This photo was one of the most used photos in
Devon and Cornwall Police.

Sometimes, photo's just
come together!

A couple of weeks later, John and I received a call from the FIM again. "Carjacking Harry" the FIM said with some genuine concern. Sometimes you have jobs you pretty much know are going to end in a nothing job where we are just there as a contingency, and others you know are the real deal. A car had been test-driven from a garage in Newton Abbot. The salesman has sat in the passenger seat with the potential customer in the driver's seat with the keys. The potential customer became a confirmed armed robber when he produced a gun, pointed it across his lap at the salesman and said, "I'll take it from here".

The helicopter was searching the area and soon traced the car, a red Citroen and was following it onto the A38 towards Plymouth giving updates as they monitored it. John and I were en route managing to squeeze 150mph out of the Volvo, with the wind behind us and downhill. We had to catch it.

The latest information was the car had stopped in a lay-by, the subject has run across the dual carriageway without a care of getting knocked over and into the bushes the other side, still with sidearm in hand. We were 5 minutes from the scene. Things were warming up a bit, as well as the atmosphere, the weather was warming up too, a beautiful blue sky framed the approaching scene of dual carriageway, hillside and woodland. As John drove the car through the rolling countryside, even though the speeds were so high, it felt idyllic, a Postman Pat countryside with toy farmhouses with miniature cows and sheep in the distance.

"There it is" Shouts John, startling me out of my daydream. He slams the car over into the lay-by behind the stolen car. We know the plan. The helicopter has traced him up to the top of the hill where he's waiting with the gun in his right hand. It's standing off for obvious reasons but videoing the whole process. John and I are out of the car digging our weapons out of the safe and with MP5's strapped across our chests, dart across the first two lanes, climb the central reservation and then pick our spot to get across the second two lanes. I can only wonder what the motorists must have thought.

Getting the earpiece ripped out of my ear by the thick bushes wasn't ideal. I located the end of it and stuffed it back in my ear catching the end of a sentence from the helicopter observer. "Can you repeat please, what's the update?". The observer in the helicopter tells me no change, the subject is pacing up and down looking agitated, as if waiting. Is this going to be death by cop?

It's a steep climb through the empty field with weapons in front stretched out towards the top of the hill only to find however, another brow of a hill to climb, it's hot and tiring. John and I are parallel to each other about 50 metres apart. We finally find the blue sky coming lower and lower to meet the grass and there in the distance about 50 metres in front of John and me, a lone dark figure standing there now motionless with a pistol in his right hand pointing towards his feet. He's wearing a dark anorak unzipped at the front, revealing a scruffy white T-shirt. Jeans and trainers finished off his outfit. What the hell was going on? Literally anything could happen in the next 10 minutes.

151

With John in my periphery view, we proceeded gingerly towards the male with the red dot in my sights jogging around the white T-shirt of the man in front of me. Just a little closer and we can start to negotiate. The male said nothing. He had pale skin and had a shaved head. He looked as though he'd had a tough life. His expression was one of resignation. It alarmed me. Viewing him through my gun sights I was concerned. He wasn't acting as he should. Let's not rush this one. He's stolen a car at gunpoint; he's abandoned it and run to the top of a hill. He's motionless but not reacting to our presence, and he still has a gun in his hand. No threat at the moment but if he raises it towards John or myself, I'm going to shoot him, and the training we have had would probably mean another bullet would be shot from John's gun instantaneously. The next few seconds were everything.

I knew we were now close enough. I shouted to the man. "We are armed police. I need you to drop that gun on the grass. Do you understand?" ...nothing. The man's head was slumped down, his shoulders drooping, his gun looking as forlorn as the rest of him. Was he crazy? Was he trying to lure us in, was this suicide by cop? I ask myself again. I believed it was the latter and I knew the next few seconds could be analysed for the next few years if things developed in a bad way. And then all of a sudden, the gun just fell to the ground as if it were an apple from a tree. No change in posture from the male, nothing, no response, just that.

It flashed through my mind to approach him and arrest him with John covering me but then it dawned on me. We are both there together. Would he think I had stolen his arrest again? There was no reason why he wouldn't think that. Was I just too pushy? Did I trample over people to get what I wanted? A crazy concern at this stage, I suggested to myself.

After a short pause, I steadied my stance and said clearly and concisely, "John, this one's yours mate, cover on"

I'm sure I could feel surprise coming from John, maybe in the momentary hesitation that John took before walking forward, myself still with my weapon raised, the red dot not leaving my view darting around the man's chest still and before we knew it John was cuffing the subject. The job was done, and we both silently realised this was a close one. This was one which could have changed our careers, our lives forever. It was highly believed the man had been institutionalised in prison and having been released, he preferred his life in prison but he wanted to do it properly and ensure it was for a long time.

If it had turned out differently however, the best barristers would have come out of the woodwork to act on behalf of the family. They would have spent months asking why this couldn't have been prevented in the first place. Could the officers just have held off? Did the helicopter scare him so did he react differently than if it hadn't been there, were the officers too keen to pull the trigger? The families would have insisted their beloved father, grandfather, son was the apple in their eye who wouldn't have hurt a fly and the police were just out for a kill, blood thirsty, careless, reckless and the media would have lapped it up and worst of all

153

John and I wouldn't have been able to defend ourselves in the public eye until years had gone by and only when all had lost interest. Even when there was found to be a lawful killing, the Independent Police Complaints Commission as then, would have taken the ear of the family. Each "no case to answer" would have been appealed, dragging this sorry affair into years of stagnant career for John and myself. No chance of promotion as it continued, no chance of looking into the future. Just waiting for the clock to tick by and wondering if the next attack by the hungry wolves would be successful.

And when the whole thing was over, probably 6 or so years later, when the interest had long died away, we would be proven absolutely correct in all we did. But it would mean nothing. It would have already destroyed us as it does so many others before us.

16. @DC_ARVSgt – Twitter

It was a complete accident. I had no intentions at all of starting a Twitter account for the police. I did have a private one I started several years before in 2009. I used it because I thought it would be quite good to stalk Formula 1 drivers and their managers to get information straight from the horse's mouth. I wasn't interested in anyone following me. It was for purely selfish means.

The short version is I put a road safety video out which went pretty much viral which celebrities then retweeted, which online papers published and I was asked by my work to decide whether to continue with a private account or to start an official police one as the two were bleeding across. The journey to that point is a bit more lengthy however, and I start with my private account with about 200 followers on it.

I was always fascinated with the world of management in Formula 1. You had your brash managers like Flavio Briatore from Benetton and later Renault who seemed to get the job done one way or another, whose drivers more feared than respected him maybe or respected him through fear, and there was Ross Brawn from Honda, Brawn and then Mercedes who came across as a wise owl, experienced who never raised his voice past whisper level... and boy did he get the job done, many a trophy proves that. I would compare this with policing management styles and often dismiss certain management courses as far too rigid. Some academic somewhere proved this is how you do this with this sort of performance development-type talk.

My experience showed you could only teach someone to manage so far, but if they haven't got it, if they cannot instil discipline and motivation naturally, then they will probably struggle for ever. This is why it's always grated me that those interviews for police promotion and no doubt most other business promotion boards, often depend on what is said on the day, the key words, and the political correctness spewing from all orifices. Little of the genuine person is learned or understood. A little unfair perhaps and I suspect I am out of date slightly as I am only getting my information third hand now and I suspect it's improving somewhat. We haven't had some odd results for a couple of years so I hope things have got better.

I digress of course, which is a usual problem of mine. Talking about something and finding something far more interesting to talk about mid-sentence! Following F1 I learned a lot. Probably far more than courses I attended. I have a unique management style which certainly doesn't appear in any manual or academic study. I tell my officers I will back them all the way however difficult things get, as long as they are not dishonest, completely negligent or malicious. And they know this because I regularly prove it to them which means they can work with freedom of fear, confident to make mistakes and for things to go wrong, but having the satisfaction knowing they have been given the freedom to make mistakes but inevitably succeed in so many other ways. There's a line between supervisor and friend of course. If I saw a couple of mine having a quick chat by the cars when they had been sent to a car broken down in a dangerous location, a regular call

156

which could soon become monotonous, I would ask, "Stood down were you guys?"

They'd reply, "No, Sarge, just going now"

I ask, "Would you still be here if it were your mother or sister in that car?" Point taken.

I was always a little bit crazy, I am sure they will agree. Coming into the parade room was like entering the stage for me, it was my theatre as well as a place to type, to relax, to polish boots, to chat before the official briefing begun. I would often drag myself in on an early turn. Up at 5.30am on a cold winter morning. I'd park my car or my motorbike in the Head Quarters car park and trudge with head down towards the door wondering how the hell I was going to summon even an ounce of motivation. I'd take a breath of cold damp air, open the door and walk in. "Right you Bastards, I want you to work today, you've had it far too easy for far too long!" Not the usual motivational speech some would give or would be recommended, but with a beaming grin over my face it or words like it would inject an energy into the room where officers would then start to discuss what they could do that shift. It picked things up. You can't teach it, god forbid that would be a disaster, but I guess it comes down to confidence.

That is worth so much more than being able to spout keywords. Keywords to a victim are an insult. Someone said to me recently, "You'd finish those forms quicker if you didn't adlib so much". I think it's a sad state of affairs if there is now so much admin to do there is no time to talk or listen, to make a victim of

157

domestic abuse feel safe, not to feel stupid and not to feel like a statistic. It's now all about telling someone we are here to ensure their safeguarding, to ensure other agencies are there to help. All this is correct but makes the whole situation into a business transaction. "This is for your Safeguarding, sign here" and on to the next job. That's never been me and never will. Listening to someone and making them feel normal is so important and that takes time.

My F1 Twitter stalking account remained pretty quiet. I knew I could get the instant reaction of an angered F1 driver which would have otherwise been filtered out by their media team given half the chance. I would view photos and selfies straight from the drivers, and I could if I felt the need, get into discussions about the sport I loved and sometimes may be fortunate enough to have a reply from a driver, although to be honest that wasn't my thing. But they were suddenly accessible. McLaren and Williams are my teams and although they have had a rough time of late, they do make the most beautiful cars and team clothing. Attention to detail gives them the professionalism but I wonder if sometimes they need a bit of Harry management style! I jest of course.

So how did this develop into the Twitter account I have now? It started when I was actively involved in a project called Learn2Live which I'd been a part of for several years. A lifesaving campaign for young drivers and passengers held in colleges and conference halls. It isn't the usual "Don't drive fast kids, don't have fun" which we know has little or no effect but instead is usually held somewhere on a stage. The audience are

158

shown a video of some youngsters getting ready for an evening out, going out in a car with the driver being distracted leading to a collision. The film stops and I walk on the stage in full uniform and recall an experience of a double fatal collision I attended caused by alcohol and fatigue. I then walk off stage, the film continues with the ambulance turning up on the film and then a paramedic in full gear walks on recalling their own memory of another incident. Then a fire-fighter and then... a next of kin. A mother of a deceased stands on the stage and relives the day she lost her daughter. The audience are in tears and many students have to leave the hall or theatre upset but where counsellors are on standby. It shouldn't be forgotten that some of these students may have lost friends or relatives in collisions previously so they are obviously warned beforehand but the presentation is often far more hard hitting than students expect.

Well there was a concern as these presentations were getting quite big and that if one of us couldn't make it for some reason and if there was no spare available officer to take my place, it may cause a rather vacant part in the proceedings. I was asked if I could pop into a driver training area in Exeter to have my presentation filmed. Several speakers did this. The film would be played in the presentation instead of having the police officer talk personally if they couldn't get someone else to replace them. I was nervous. The guy who'd originally brought this together in our area, Nigel Flowers, was known for ripping speeches up of new speakers, much to their horror of course. "I don't want it from this", he'd say holding the ripped papers up, "I want it from here" as he tapped the left side of his chest. He's why it works so well. He's an absolute gentleman and someone I consider to be a friend. It is why Learn2Live worked and Nigel did so much to make it work. When I tell my particular story I travel a journey through my memory and relive the incident to a certain extent. As I tell the story in my mind it would poke at new thoughts and emotions which would suddenly pop up without notice, it may not affect me too much as a professional on the whole, but could catch me out as I was suddenly thrust back to the collision site with the victim back in front of me. Feeling the cold or the heat, the wet or wind, smelling the oil, it may take me anywhere.

My talk was about a girl called Anna. She was 23 years old and she got a lift home from a party by someone she thought she could trust but who had been drinking. They had just crashed into the back of a highways truck in the early hours of the morning when I turned up. Anna was obviously dead already and I tried to treat the driver's injuries but he didn't live long once he'd been removed from the car. A tragic incident which I recall many times with my presentation but I try to vary it just a little each time to keep it real. I don't want it to become the norm, but to give respect to her memory.

The unique part to my Learn2Live story however, is Anna's mother tells her own account of that day later on in the presentation with so much effect, Anna's mother Ali Norrish is a wonderfully strong woman, kind, loving in fact beautiful in every way. The way Anna was taken away from her and her family was brutal and is one of the reasons I've been an atheist in my adult life. Not this specific incident of course, but I am happy in the thought I don't want to be a part of anyone who thinks this is alright and that suffering like this is necessary. Test or no test, they can shove their test. Worship God or you go to hell, it's a bully in the playground you have to be a friend of or he'll beat you up, well I learned how to deal with bullies.

So I have a wonderful freedom without requiring forgiveness or feeling guilty for enjoying pleasures etc. I know it was just tragic luck on Anna's part and selfish decisions by the driver that morning that changed lives forever. A set of circumstances, which could have been avoided if the driver had had more responsibility, had realised the dangers, had made other plans.

There I was dressed up in my Armed Response black uniform with all my equipment dripping off it, standing in front of a camera with an official looking woman standing next to it. She told me to look either at the camera lens or at her, and I chose her. I had no idea how this would go. I preferred to talk to a lot of people as they just became a blur in a crowd, nothing personal about them so I would talk to the fog of people. This was different, this was speaking one to one and it was freaking me out a little. The fewer people the more into your soul they can see, the more awkward things can feel. I hoped I wouldn't waste their time too much with retakes. This could be an utter nightmare but I began...

... and I spoke for 10 minutes travelling through my memories, describing what I saw as they popped up into my mind, what I was feeling, and then I began to explain how it affects the rest of the family, not just the victim. Ali had quietly walked through the door to be the next one to complete her video, and as I talked about her, I made the mistake of quickly glancing at this woman standing there in silence staring at me, listening to my words about the daughter she loved so much and lost in such a violent way. I was talking about something so personal, and I had a moment, just a frog in my throat, but I had to check myself and after a stuttering pause I collected myself and looked back at the camera to continue. I thought I'd wrecked it but I carried on and finished. I was waiting for the woman to ask me to retake parts or even all of it but as I looked at her I could see a tear running down her cheek. I asked her, "Will that do?"

"Yes" she replied. "Yes, that's perfect".

And when that video was put on YouTube by the Learn2Live team along with many others from speakers from all emergency services and family, that was the one that rocketed in views. Whereas most were hitting 500, or 2000 views even, that video went to 70,000 views, and I realised it was because the public suddenly could see we were human. Here was a police officer in the Armed Response Unit, dual roled with Traffic with kit hanging off him, trained to deal with all violent and tragic incidents just about to shed a tear. It showed he gave a shit and I think they appreciated that.

When that video was making the rounds and local online papers were publishing it, and then Philip

Schofield kindly put it on his Twitter page even waiting until after X Factor for maximum effect, I was approached by my Force to consider either changing my Twitter page to a Force one, or starting a new one for the Force. They were not comfortable with a private account talking about Police matters. They needed to have some sort of control and awareness over it. That's reasonable considering what I say may have an effect on the reputation of the Force and as I had 200 or so followers already on Twitter, I didn't fancy losing them so I changed my private account to my Force details and after a quick chat with the Force Corporate Comms department, started with my new account. I was never going to find any problems as I wasn't the sort to lose my rag or type anything stupid when I'd had a drink, and I never did, but I was soon to discover that that would not stop me getting into a whole lot of trouble on more than a few occasions.

My style of policing has always been to show a human side. It was easier than putting on a facade; my style is also quite direct. I don't see the point in faffing about when someone is out of order in, say, a domestic situation or on the high street when perhaps they've had too much to drink. By being natural, showing my human side, I could be myself as there was no acting involved and it made it easier. At first I would be nervous with my tweets, wondering if I was showing too much of my vulnerabilities but I found the reaction was incredibly positive. Follower numbers were soaring, the more I used humour, compassion, whenever I was self-deprecating, and people seemed to appreciate that especially as I was supposed to have one of the more macho jobs in the police. No, they didn't want a wimp, but they wanted to see what the person was like beneath the uniform... so to speak!

They wanted to know what annoyed me with policing aspects, what downright angered me, and they enjoyed the inside perspective when talking about police specialist subjects. Pursuits, spit hoods, mental health, firearms, fatalities, complaints, numerous subjects with an insider's point of view but with nearly 30 years' experience without an agenda, well that I could see any way!

I was fortunate to be runner up to the Police Blog Twitter awards, and was voted best Police Sergeant Twitter awards and the overall winner for 2016. This was incredible for networking as contacts are everything in this world. It is very much who you know and it's how you get things done. It means I can often find information from other police forces far more quickly than the more formal methods from within my own Force.

Winning it meant I was sent to Long Beach in LA where I gave a talk on Twitter and it was here that I noticed the USA had very similar issues in policing as we do in the UK. I still cannot believe how fortunate I've been, but I am convinced it's because people can see I am so concerned about getting policing right, about defending us from idiotic statements by press or MP's, and just as importantly for supporting police cadets, new police applicants, those across the country in other Forces wanting advice on joining Firearms, and students doing a degree in university where they ask to talk to me to help with their course-work.

I do enjoy writing blogs but I only write them when I have something to say. I found them quite easy to write as instead of thinking of what to write I just write about experiences. I wrote one on *A Diversion from my Day to Day Life* about what happens on being called to a serious collision. I just live these blogs through writing; a little bit like with my Learn2Live speech. It's important to drag the reader through the thriller with you, ensuring they feel the changes in emotion and feel the same journey as me. I was concerned it was a little cheesy at first but thought, sod it, 'publish' on the bloggers' site "WordPress" and away it went. This was my first big blog and you can find it at the end of this book. It went rather well and I knew it was pretty good much to my surprise when my much respected colleague Glen Bullock said at work as I walked into the office, "Did you write that, did you seriously right that or did you get some help with it?". I had surprised him, and that surprised me. Okay I thought, maybe it is pretty good.

These blogs got me the interest of what was then the IPCC, the Independent Police Complaints Commission, now known as the Independent Office of Police Complaints. (IOPC). A direct message from the office of the deputy commissioner requested a chat regarding a blog I did on Post Incident Shootings. There had grown mistrust with the media by police on post shootings when vicious, dangerous criminals had been shot dead by police having just thrown a gun from the car without it having been seen thrown. For some

165

unfathomably strange reason a section of society felt the armed police should risk their lives by giving these people the benefit of the doubt when they believed in that split second they were going to be shot by these animals. It was being heavily pushed for all officers involved in shootings to be segregated post shooting, great in theory, ridiculous and callous in practice. My blog took the reader through a story of a shooting and the practicalities and emotions of going through that experience under the new system. As usual, I based my blogs on true incidents often very accurately which means it's very easy for me to imagine, to tell the story as realistically as I can and so it soon got the attention of the IPCC office, but in a good way! I have published this blog near the end of this book named, *We Need You But We Don't Want You.*

I replied to the office of Sarah Green, the deputy commissioner, stating I couldn't come to London but Sarah requested I meet her in Exeter. No concerns there then!

I wondered if I was going to be flattered into silence or threatened. Time would tell. I thought it wise to tell my Force of my meeting and they requested, to their credit, I have a Superintendent there, a person I very much respected who was also a Post Incident Manager of a high profile case running at that time.

The meeting took place over an orange juice in a pub near Exeter Railway station as she only had 2 hours spare. I was extremely flattered she should come all the way from London to see me and I did wonder what her agenda was. Did she seriously want to have a better idea? Was I being too suspicious? As I spent more time with her I found her to be a very nice lady. I told her I had wanted to dislike her as that would have made things much easier, which she laughed at, but I did also have an extremely open honest discussion with her regarding the treatment of officers post shootings. Just to separate the key witnesses would often have required hiring out a Holiday Inn due to the numbers involved, and the wait would have been for several hours, basically kept in solitary confinement, completely inhumane under the circumstances. My blog was called, *We Need You But We Don't Want You* and I am sure it was a coincidence but the appetite for segregation soon diminished except for in some extreme circumstances where a crime by officers was suspected.

I felt Sarah did listen but it looked clear to me the basics for an independent view was missing. I remember she said, "You see, Harry, I want the public to know they CAN trust the police" and I remember her surprise when I said, "But you are killing officers by proving that, I prefer you didn't prove that to the public but the officers could live their lives instead of having them on hold for years on end."

I am extremely clear about this. We don't treat our worst, most dangerous criminals like we treat our police officers being investigated. The Human Rights Act decrees that every state should have a proportionate investigation into every death of one of its citizens. Sounds great but our country ignores the word proportionate and for many years decided to treat officers like murder suspects but over a much longer period of time than you would be able to legally treat a genuine murder suspect. Whereas investigations often must be over in days for criminal offences, where police are involved it can drag into 4, 5, 6 years with endless appeals by families of complainants. One case of assault recently came to light dragged into a 10 year process when a layman could have told you there was no evidence after just a couple of months. I feel the IOPC is still heavily influenced by the extremely loud complainants and our politically correct world we live in means they are listened to at the huge expense and injustice to the officer, who are considered irrelevant. Ultimately these people live by the sword and the chances are they can die by the sword. Get over it and don't take it out on the officers doing exactly as society has demanded they do on their behalf.

Too many activists or certain MP's with dubious backgrounds and abusive natures are given a pedestal to spew their bile on how corrupt the police are and how for example this poor young man was killed by the nasty police. The fact this poor young man was a drug dealer and user who robbed from the public every opportunity he had and was simply caught and died through his own lifestyle, is of little interest to a fair society until after the inquest. The fact the poor young man choked on something he swallowed to hide the evidence, or his heart stopped because of the cocaine in his system whilst in custody is always thrown at the blame of the police. Always a promising footballer, a promising singer, just a lost soul who went down the wrong path, probably because it was the one of least resistance, but nevertheless should not be one to blame on the police and these activists to make a living from like the vultures they are.

I had to be careful because my twitter posts were becoming more to do with national police issues such as assault, complaints against police and debates on body-worn video, spit hoods and Taser. I found I was able to talk more on these subjects whereas so many other officers, especially in London were unable to. I didn't kid myself, I was sure I was an extremely insignificant part of all of this debate, but I was secretly surprised how I was able to continue the way I did. What gave me immense strength were the direct messages from officers, often Armed Response Officers and Traffic Officers who sent messages such as, "Thank you Harry, thank you for making us look human". That sentence meant so much, because if I didn't have the respect of my colleagues whatever Force they were in, then it was time to stop.

I was always surprised I didn't get throwback comments from people saying, "What do you know in Devon and Cornwall?" I never did. I suppose it is quite rare to have someone on the front line for 30 years, and of those 25 years being on Firearms and specialising with fatal road traffic collisions. That did give me some credibility I guess but when officers contacted me with appreciative comments from the Metropolitan Forces or from specialist departments such as Collision Investigation, Traffic or ARV, that meant so much. I knew I was hitting the mark. The last thing I wanted to do was to make a fool of myself, my colleagues or the police force as a whole.

I realised the strength of Twitter when subjects such as #BrewsForBlues surfaced. I have more conversations going on in Direct Messages and groups which are behind the scenes of my public profile of Twitter, than I do on the public arena of Twitter itself. I do not use Twitter just for the social side of it, to be honest I am very bad at the polite chat that so many involve themselves in. I use it to advance the truth and credibility of policing, to highlight the issues police face that is so regularly conveniently avoided by the press. So when a paper picked up on officers having a tea break together on the seafront at Plymouth with their cars parked in a long row opposite their cafe, the photo hit the national press with an underlying message of how these officers should have been working harder on a Sunday morning and could not be quite as overworked as they say they were.

I, with a very select band of 'Twitterers' got to work to provide the truth behind the headline: that being there are no longer any canteens, they were likely to be debriefing from a traumatic incident such as a fatal road traffic collision, a cot death, a suicide or a complicated incident where a thorough debrief was required or indeed it could have simply been just because they hadn't stopped all week and the Sergeant had called everyone together to have a bit of rest and recuperation. The cars were so numerous as they'd all been single-crewed, and it also meant they were free to attend any emergency at the drop of a hat.

The hashtag #BrewsForBlues was devised by some wise person amongst us and what was meant as a negative bash against the police turned quickly into an incredibly positive story. I would put a tweet I devised into the private room with my contacts of many who would retweet it and I would do likewise with theirs if it felt relevant. This way we soon had a reach of half a million people in a very short time. That's the power of Twitter, not manipulating the facts, just getting them out there, and very soon I found the diet for slagging police officers off with fake stories soon diminished as the public were quickly given the truth behind the headlines. We finally had a voice, and it felt good. The bosses were coming out of the woodwork too, all over the country supporting the officers having breaks and Chief Constables were encouraging officers to do likewise for their mental health. And now we hear of press receiving photos from the public of officers having a break in McDonalds and instead of trying to embarrass the officers, they are now supporting them against the unscrupulous photographer.

What I can say is how utterly supportive my Chief Constable Shaun Sawyer and Deputy Chief Constable Paul Netherton have been in all my time using Twitter. I still don't know how I haven't worn their patience down but they have stuck by me way back from the time I was talking to a domestic violence victim and was trying to encourage her to come to the police for support. One of the numerous tweets in the thread I sent was that she was the adult and, even though he treated her as a child to control her, she could find the strength to make the first step to leave him or seek help. I encouraged her to make a stand. This completely backfired, not with her who completely understood my point but by onlookers who quickly warped my intentions. There were quickly screenshots of the very insular tweet with the caption of "This officer still works?" A typical "pull yourself together attitude", which quickly got taken on by others and before I knew it no one was reading what I had written but instead what others had said I had written and their interpretations of it. This is typical in the social media world when people have an axe to grind. Those people who are so angry at the police because they haven't been able to wave a magic wand to fix an age old problem of theirs overnight, they just wanted to blame them for its cause even, and I was the easy target.

Complaints inevitably arrived at the door of my HQ which meant time spent dealing with them by my complaints department, my Corporate Comms and my Supervisor and each time I had the stress of talking to them to discuss ways forward. We would try to agree on how we could try to avoid it in future however several complaints later when all, in my mind, were a result of having a few haters amongst a large number of followers, I had to tell them I couldn't guarantee it wouldn't happen again. The important point however was they could tell I was trying to avoid trouble, and none of my complaints were through being unprofessional or angry, they were things that people just were ignorant of or simply just disagreed with.

Vicky Goodwin was my Corporate Comms boss for a long period of time and I would receive a text from her asking when I was next in. I knew it was about some bad news regarding another complaint. I remember being fed up as someone who had an agenda was using a complaint to have a go and I knew it. I also knew I had let my guard down and had allowed it to happen. I was angry with myself as I sat in her office with her talking over some potential solutions, with her trying to reduce the workload on her staff I was causing in such a balanced manner, I found her incredibly understanding. So much so when I came into her office she sat and we chatted and something happened to me. I just couldn't stop the tears flowing. Highly embarrassing for me to admit, as I can say I hadn't cried for decades but I'd had enough and I'd put this poor woman in a rather awkward position to say the least! She was very kind and supportive, I think if not rather taken aback but I realised it was getting too much for me. What the hell was I doing this for? Why was I doing this Twitter? As she constantly reminded me, I was getting 99% right but it was only the odd tweet that was backfiring. I was doing it as I was getting results, I was talking to MP's on topics I could educate them about and I was speaking to influential people to get these things on TV discussion programs. In other words getting the truth out there and that was satisfying after 30 years of working at ground level. I was getting results higher up and that felt good.

My Chief, Shaun Sawyer rang me at home on a couple of occasions to see how I was coping after a number of press bashings. I kept his number in my phone after the first call and each time I was recovering from a recent Twitter and online paper backlash on what *Controversial Police Sergeant Tangye* had said, the Chief Constable's name would come up on my phone. I would have a minor panic thinking the worst and yet some warm words came flowing over that phone line. "Hello Harry, Shaun here, I just wanted to call you to see how you are after today". An amazing genuine man and I owe him so much for that.

The Command Team shared the same canteen in HQ with everyone else and after yet another issue over a topic the local press had picked up on, even I was thinking I had tried their patience once too often. I would see Deputy Chief Paul Netherton walk through the door and I would quietly hide at the other side of the canteen in case I suddenly caught his disapproving gaze! The next thing I knew he was marching over to me with his hand open for a handshake with his beaming smile spread across his face. "Hello Harry, I see you're in trouble again!". He would be chuckling a mischievous laugh. He'd then follow this up with some incredibly encouraging words for which I am forever grateful. These two men in particular have been so supportive over the years. They've understood I was hopefully doing more good than harm, but I realised it was a support most other officers in other Forces didn't have the luxury of and I had to ensure I didn't let them down.

And then there is my constant staple source of advice and wisdom, that being from Mike Pannett, someone I now consider a great friend who has saved my sanity on more than one occasion. He's ex-services, ex-police and current successful author and Director. He's been a true friend indeed to whom I'm forever indebted. It's strange you can meet someone just a handful of times and become great friends but Twitter has linked us pretty much daily on important topics going on around the country. He will often organise some support for some deserving need and before you know it, the subject's trending. His contacts are phenomenal and I have no doubt he has contributed massively to the Police Service that no one will ever know.

17. What Lengths To Save a Man's Life?

I'm single-crewed screaming my marked X5 through the streets, looking far ahead to see if I should start braking now or whether it is clear enough to maintain my momentum. The call says it's a motorcycle and a pedestrian involved and they are not looking good. I've quickly worked out that I'm going to be the first police unit there. Another call says it's really serious and I'm told that ambulance won't be there for some time. It's rare when you realise you are definitely going to be the first on scene with no officers or paramedics. It gives me time to prepare as I wind myself through the queue at the traffic lights, and turn sharp left onto the long road leading towards the scene. The checklist pops up into my mind. Stop the car in the best place, protect the scene, run to rear nearside door, that's where the first aid bag is, run to boot to get the oxygen stacked above the armoury, get to first casualty, don't get sucked in, check both casualties if there are and delegate for the minor injury, I'll deal with the major one.

I see it in the distance. A motorbike laying on the road and two small groups about 10 metres apart, crowding around their points of interest. I slew the X5 across the middle of the road and run to the rear nearside door, grab the first aid bag, collect the oxygen and within seconds am running to the first group. It's the biker in leathers and he has an open fracture on his left shin, otherwise looks okay but he's not responding to me when I ask him his name. I run over to the other male and find an elderly but thick-set gentleman sitting up chatting. I'm confused at the order of severity of injuries, I'd have expected worse from him so I return to the biker. I remove his helmet as he's struggling to breathe.

ARV medical training is good because it's practical and regular so it gives you confidence in a crisis. We realise how good when we get assessed sometimes alongside regular officers who do not have that training.

Someone at the scene queries, "Should we be removing that helmet?"

"It's the first thing that'll kill him at the moment if I don't as he's struggling for breath. If he was breathing easily then we leave it."

I put the oxygen on him and turned the two valves of life to feed the brain with the oxygen it is so badly wanting. If he has an internal injury he may have less blood in his system so if what he has is richer in oxygen, this gives him more time. I look around me, get confirmation the other chap is doing okay so pull the heavy duty scissors from my kit and cut up the legs and arms of his leathers. "He won't like me for this" I exclaimed. I hoped he would get the chance to curse me later anyway.

He's exposed in his boxer shorts and I assess him for further injuries, feeling every part I can't see hidden behind and checking my plastic gloves for blood, then move on, looking for deformities in his torso but nothing. He's now kicking his legs and his wound is opening from the fracture so I gently try to restrain the movement on that leg. I know it's a head injury now because of his outbursts, and suddenly a couple of paramedics arrive. I don't even hear the air ambulance arrive just metres away from me in a local sports field across the road, but at the moment my work is done on the medical side and so I step back to speak to some witnesses leaving the experts to it.

I established the pedestrian stepped out in front of the bike and the motorcyclist came off hitting his head on a metal safety bar on the rear of an oncoming lorry which was fortunately stationary. That explains the head injury then.

The Hems Doctor working with the motorcyclist shouts for my assistance. "We need to move fast. He's haemorrhaging somewhere fast and we need to stop it. He'll be dead by the time we get him to the heli!"

With the assistance of some other paramedics and technicians, we got him onto the scoop, a stretcher in two parts lengthways to make it easier to place under the casualty. Then on to the trolley but instead of heading for the air ambulance we are heading another 10 metres to the shelter of the motorway bridge above. It has started to rain and if the doctor was to open him up, the less distractions the better. It was daylight but still quite gloomy with the heavy clouds above that had just begun to release their heavy load of water. The road was cordoned off nicely but there were insistent pedestrians trying to get through with minimal officers available to stop them. We were hoping the blue and white police tape would be enough to persuade them to turn back.

What he did then was nothing short of remarkable. He carried out what's called an emergency Thoracotomy. He drew his scalpel across the man's chest from nipple to nipple, used scissors to cut the line deeper, and then used a wire saw to cut through the sternum. The chest was then cranked up from the head side and a senior nurse massaged the heart whilst the casualty was fully intubated. This gave time for the doctor to move organs around with his hands to look for the wound that was releasing so much blood into the chest. My job was to... hold the torch... so he could have a good look into the more gloomy crevices of the body around the back of the lung etc. I knew that now was not the time to drop it.

Scanning a casual look around me to take in this surreal scene I had suddenly been thrust into, I noticed 2 boys in their early teens pushing a cycle along the path coming straight towards us. Clearly they wanted to get past and thought if they walked their bikes they would be free to pass. This is the universal sign to show "we mean no harm". What they didn't realise is they were very quickly going to see a scene from a horror movie that may possibly affect the rest of their lives. I shouted at them to turn back as it wasn't very pleasant and I think the message was immediately received as their shocked faces took in the scene from a distant 25 metres or so. They spun their bikes around their heels and meekly made their way back towards the police tape again.

I hoped the doctor would exclaim in delight and put his finger into a hole that would save the patient's life. When these procedures are carried out in the field as a last resort so to speak, they are done as a last resort but it is known to have a 20% success rate. What I can say is that lad had been given every chance. We all so wanted him to survive but the doctor found too many internal lacerations and he bled out too quickly. It did show however it had been the right call. He would have certainly died before he'd been safely strapped in the helicopter.

I am fascinated in this emergency treatment. I love being tested practically. When others freeze, it's a joy to see others cracking on. If I am in the position of a patient or relative relying on others so much, I want to see the confidence on the faces of those coming to assist. I want to see them cracking on to help my loved one. It's so important so you know everything is being carried out as best it can with experience, expertise and professionalism so I've always made an effort to get as proficient in first aid as I can.

18. How Hard Can it be to Shoot Right?

I'd entered the world of policing as you already know, with a feeling in my guts that I was a complete fraud and one day someone would find me out. Every day was more fun than the previous, but I felt very young indeed at the time, I lacked experience but I soon gained it through all those jobs and incidents I attended and from absorbing wisdom from my wonderful tutors who spilled their pearls of wisdom. I was in awe of them all!

As my confidence grew, I decided I most definitely wanted to join the Firearms Unit. This consisted back then of storing your weapons at the station armoury which were then logged out when there was an incident. I remember seeing a couple of plain cars leaving Torquay police station full of weapon brandishing officers. This looked so cool and I was transfixed, I thought nothing could get anymore cool, however I think I was also very easily impressed at the age of 22! After 8 years or so in the Service I applied for the Firearms department which meant I would still stay on Response but I would be on the call out register and be issued with an even more *I'm very important* pager. I was quite nervous as the Inspector in charge of Firearms was quite a foreboding chap. He never had too much to say to me when I nervously attempted to make conversation with him which will have sounded like a nervous chat-up line at the school disco. I don't think I impressed him much!

My whole career in Firearms almost ended before it had even started. I was a passenger in a patrol car with my very good friend the now Sgt Olly Tayler QPM. This began when we realised the patrol cars had a PA system on them we hadn't known about until very recently. Having chosen a reasonably quiet piece of road I decided to try out my Star Wars Obi-Wan impression across half of Torbay. This was quite impressive and I had previously got quite a reaction when I had tried it in bars and Police Vans using the cups of my hands to cover my mouth for greatest effect. It didn't take a lot to entertain me then, or now if I am perfectly honest so I clicked the transmit button and the following came forth in deep Star Wars type voices... "Obi-Wan, you fight well; your father has taught you well."

I beamed a huge grin of satisfaction in this moment of self-gratification but which very quickly changed to utter terror when I saw the Firearms Inspector standing on the pavement no more than 50 metres in front of me having just stopped and spoken to a member of the public. The answer to my future career was standing before me staring at our car and slowly walking towards us with his hand raised up to stop us. He bent down through the passenger window and paused in that terrifying superior Inspector sort of way, then said, "Gentlemen, could we possibly have a bit of professionalism please?"

My quivering reply, "Yes Sir" must have sounded pathetic. He had spoken to me in a way very much like 'You've disappointed me, you've disappointed the whole school, and most of all you've let yourself down'. Surely I wouldn't get through the paper sift now. How could he trust me with a car PA, let alone a gun!

Well, for some unknown reason, I got through the paper sift and onto the 3 day assessment course to be selected for the next stage. Things didn't get off to a flying start as I may have got the timings a little wrong for driving to HQ from my home address this being before the days of Google maps and therefore I realised half-way having sat in traffic jams for most of it, I had badly misjudged the travelling time. I was going to be late for the induction to the course which meant my day couldn't have gone any worse. I finally turned up at the range classroom out of breath from running from my half abandoned Metro in the car park and found the door locked. I nervously walked over to the classroom windows and tapped on the window to be let into the secure classroom. All eyes were on me, I knew what they were all thinking, 'Great stuff, he's one down already!' I knew from now on I had nothing to lose. I had to prove my metal because I was already in the bin and it was up to me to climb out of it.

I did need to tell a white lie about breaking down. I had to give the instructors something to hang on to so I don't feel my integrity was completely lacking even though I'm sure they didn't believe me for a second. The three days were tough, a lot in snow blizzards I remember and on Woodbury Common carrying heavy things through very wet, cold and muddy things, with memory tests and other assessments. It also involved sitting on containment in the driving snow at the other end of the field to call in every movement in the accommodation block opposite. This became farcical when the snow shower obliterated the whole building so we couldn't see the whole of HQ, let alone a window with a man wearing a mask walking from the left to right!

At the end of the three days I walked into the interview with three on the board including "the Inspector". This was it, decision time and I knew I was up against it. I sat uncomfortably on the seat trying to make out as if I wasn't too concerned with the outcome, but then seconds later thinking perhaps this was the wrong impression to give and perhaps I should give the impression of being more earnest. Whatever I thought the decision was already made and there was nothing I could do to change it so I sat there... and then thought perhaps this is one of those interviews where it was make or break. Now perhaps I'm thinking too much so I thought to hell with it, I shall just answer the questions.

It seemed to be going well but I soon realised this was a bit of a recap interview really, to give me an answer one way or another and I knew I had done everything I could. Then the Inspector began to talk and he looked stern. I have to give it to that man, that Inspector told me he had done everything he possibly could to get me off the course. He had taken me out of the paper sift but I was put back on at the last minute and having spoken for a couple of minutes he smiled and told me I had proved him wrong. I was in. Wow. I owe you Inspector Tony Ivey. You gave me the benefit of the doubt and you changed my life.

The course itself was 8 weeks long if I remember correctly. I do remember I couldn't shoot for toffee and calling my wife on the phone saying, "Do you know, love, maybe it just isn't my thing". I remember her comforting words, but I was getting 37 or 39 out of 50 on the qualification shoots when I needed at least 45 to pass. The final day of the course would be when the pressure was on. 50 shots in various exercises, and if 45 of them weren't where they should be the 8 weeks will have been for nothing.

There was another officer on my course who I had a natural utmost respect for. His name was Adam Gee and he is still one of my best friends. He smoked roll ups; he used to be in the merchant navy working himself up to second captain before joining the police for two years before returning back to sea, and before returning to the police again. Think of your sea-hardened blaggard and you have Adam! The most gravelly of voices and the filthiest dirty laugh which could have been confused for Sid James, with a vocabulary that had no filter! But what that man did was show me how to relax. To not stress over things that couldn't be changed, but to be professional to the core and to do one's very best. He gave me composure and made me laugh when I wouldn't have otherwise. This man's professionalism paid off when he was in charge of organising numerous Royal Visits having been an Authorised Firearms Officer on the ARV's for some time. He's a man who could mix with the cleaner as much as the future King of England. Everyone needs an Adam!

6 weeks into the course and I'm still struggling. I was lying prone at a quarry we use for training and I had a Glock semi automatic pistol in my hands. A giant of a man in stature, but not necessarily in height stood

behind me. He had red hair and a bushy ginger moustache and was called Ginge strangely enough. He had a booming voice to suit and we all respected him and secretly quite feared him. He is a lovely guy to whom I am eternally grateful. I shot a round and it obviously wasn't good. "Tangye, ease that trigger. Once that finger starts pulling, imagine there's a cog in it and you can't stop it. The gun should go off as a surprise, and then you know you haven't snatched it."

I could feel the breeze flowing through the quarry, there was the odd bird fluttering through the trees just the far side of the targets. Even they can't have thought much of my accuracy and fancied their chances of dodging the odd bullet for the prize of a butterfly that had landed on top of the *"Leave as you find it"* sign. I put the tension on the trigger and kept pulling gently, imagining the cogs in my knuckles rotating. There was nothing I could do… "BANG" off it went unexpectedly.

"SHIT", I think to myself, "that one must have gone wide, it just went off".

"Bang on, Tangye, nice shot, do that again." That quarry was the place Ginge, or John Gingell, taught me to shoot amongst several others for sure, but it all happened with Ginge for me. The sun came out, the angels sang, all became clear, I could shoot. 2 weeks later, on my final assessment shoot, I shot 50 out of 50. Job done.

25 years later, I am still shooting. I love having the skill and I get the same feeling I imagine as someone playing golf for the weekend. We do things that stag-

dos would pay hundreds to do, but then they don't quite have the pressure behind it except personal pride. Be it the covert holster on VIP protection or the ARV holster for Armed Response, I love the art of drawing fast and slickly, firing one or two for the desired discipline, checking breach to ensure no stoppage has occurred and then down into the holster again without looking. Fast, slick, professional and disciplined is what it's about, and boy does it feel good when you manage it in seconds. There is always a personal ego to get the first shot off but balanced with the fact you can't miss a shot. Many of these scenarios may be something such as 15 metres, 3 seconds to draw your Glock, 2 body shots on target one, 2 on target two body, and then 2 on head of target 1. So satisfying when it goes well!

Okay, I may have a little fun. There is no reason at all why the Sergeant should be better shots than his officers but there is the obvious competition between all, and especially between the Sergeant and the PC's. There are usually 24 officers shooting for an ARV refresher but only 12 lanes so there are two serials that undertake the shoot. I like to get into the second one to learn the timings, in other words, yes we know it's 3 seconds to draw, fire 2 at the body and one to the head but how fast does that look in reality. Move fast, shoot slow, and so I perfected a very fast draw which has given me another quarter of a second to get that aim in right. Without getting too technical for those that aren't interested in shooting, you have to line the single white dot at the front of the pistol, the foresight, with the centre of the 2 white dots, the rear sites. I found instead of looking at the dot, I would try to equalise the very slim gap either side of the foresight with the rear sights. Just one millimetre off with the Glock, (a snatch of a trigger) will pull a round 13 millimetres off a target at 20 metres, so you see there isn't too much room for error. Getting them all on is one thing, but getting a neat group is quite another.

It must be like playing golf I imagine in more ways than one other than just enjoyment, you can easily forget exactly how much effort is put into each and every shot. The stance of your feet, breathing, trigger tension, foresight sharp, target slightly blurred and squeeeeeeeze, and repeat that 4 times adjusting your aim to 2 separate targets within 4 seconds. It's fun, but it takes immense concentration.

But when I've been on the first serial and am happy with my score, I would often walk past one of my section who was just lining up nervously, and I'd say, "Remember... don't balls it up!". Okay, I wasn't nasty enough to do that to someone who was struggling that day, but certainly if they were on to a clean sheet and had a chance of beating me! After all, I can't have them beating the Sergeant, right! In the interests of fair play however, I would forgive them the odd, "Bastard Sarge!" under their breath!

19. Never Sit In The Comfortable Seat

I decided from the beginning of my career to take on the advice of one of my tutors: "Never turn down a course". So I volunteered for all courses given out at briefing and I got most of them. Most would be things such as Interview Courses and Public Order Unit Courses, and it taught me not to be shy of putting myself forward into an area of the unknown.

Within Firearms I was happy with my lot and thought that perhaps I had done my last course, but how naive I was. You already know it took two goes to pass my interview to join the police and now I had joined the firearms team I was putting myself through the driving courses. I passed the Standard and pursuit courses but then failed the final assessment for the Advanced. "No sparkle", he said, 'I'd have expected more from a Standard Course'. I had just kept my head down to stay out of trouble but it hadn't been enough, so a week later I planted the accelerator until I had more sparkle coming from that car than a Millennium New Year's night in London! He got sparkle as I drove that car like I stole it. The course was duly passed which meant I could carry on in Firearms on the Armed Response Unit. ARV was like a game of snakes and ladders, gradually pass all the courses but fail just one and you are dropped down the bottom and out of the door. No second go. I could remain on a department such as Neighbourhood or Response and choose not to undertake any courses if I wished. No refresher courses or assessments to stress me out but that would be boring right? But I had one life and I wanted to wring the hell out of it so I certainly didn't want to be stuck in an office with a blue folder to take out to my next meeting. Ye Gods, no.

I never thought I would be interested in being a Firearms Tactics Advisor. Why would I want to be in that office with the boss and me giving all those critical tactics as advice when I could be smashing down those doors sticking guns in nasty people's faces? Well I soon realised I wanted both and the excitement from helping to put together a plan, thinking of all the contingencies and being valued as an experienced officer by a Superintendent was quite incredible. When you were waiting for the team to go in, the room would be on tenterhooks, and the relief was just as powerful as if you had been there at that location. When you hear the words, "2 subjects arrested, no casualties, and no team casualties" you know it's a good job well done.

I had been promoted down to the City of Plymouth, an 80 mile round trip. They didn't mess around in those days! My motorbike was my mode of transport and chucking down a tube of energy sweets before riding back at 4am probably wasn't the safest mode of transport but it was the only one available to me at the time.

Having successfully managed to find my way back into Firearms after almost 3 years of Response work in Plymouth I eventually undertook an Operational Firearms Commanders (OFC) course. Basically a team leader and something I was very happy doing but this course was professionalising it. I, like many get very nervous when being assessed and start wondering what

190

they are after and often do something because of this I wouldn't normally do. So you can imagine how devastated I was when I failed the course on one of the final assessments. Especially as it was a 5-day course with long days and nights of study.

How could I be an Armed Response Sergeant and not be OFC? I realised if I failed another course that would be it. I'd have to find another role somewhere, but there was nothing that attracted me. After three or so months I was put on another course run by another Force, long days and nights, a completely different shape to the course, and just as hard. I was listening to others saying there was no way they would do it again if they failed. I tutted to myself wondering why I was crazy enough to do so but here I was. I flew through it and got my wings, so to speak.

I had also failed the new building search system brought in. I was pulled out with several others who had been in a while with several systems in their heads and put through to another week's course. Fail it a second time and I'm off. More pressure but I did it and by day two the penny had dropped and I was skipping through the hallways without a care in the world and I passed it without a problem. In 30 years policing there have been several other occasions when I have asked myself why I don't do a job within the police that didn't constantly test me. I wouldn't be so flippant to say an easier life, but one where I didn't have to put half my chips on red and only have one more go if I lost. The saying in Firearms you often hear is "Think of the extra money". Well, we all know there isn't any. We do it for the love of the job.

I often tell new officers about my failings. As a probationer I remember looking up at the Firearms Sergeant who was also the Traffic Sergeant thinking, 'Wow, he must be good', doubting my own abilities would ever match theirs. How it would have given me encouragement if I had known how many times things had gone badly for them too. The fact you give something another go means you already have experience in that skill above the others on the second course. Don't be the one who wanders off bitter and twisted saying the world is against them. "Never sit in the comfortable seat".

20. Bravery

What does it mean to be brave? People have tried to define it for many years. The meaning of courageous behaviour or character doesn't help much. Some less well-meaning people or criminals will say only the bullied in school become police officers. I guess the only part correct with that could be if you are saying the bullied had to find their own way against the odds into adulthood and they either failed or became strong but were also honest, true and found themselves. Those that did the bullying were left to decay in adulthood as they lost their fit bodies and flowing blonde hair but became fat and bald with nothing more to show for their characters.

I was one of those that always kept a bullied student under my wing and ended up getting into fights for my efforts. I had a sense of justice even then so would scrap a few times a year mainly because my cheekiness or back-chat to a much larger person who would corner me into a position I couldn't get out of.

I got frustrated at one lad I tried to help, a very skinny lad with large framed glasses who lived with his grandparents, and no doubt already hid a sad upbringing I imagined. His city worker briefcase would get thrown from one side of the classroom to the other and he'd continually be teased and made a joke of. I realised after my 3rd scrap on his behalf I was becoming a fool here as all my advice to this lad about keeping a low profile was going unheeded. That's when I realised that at some point, everyone needs to take some responsibility and at least try to help themselves a bit. It was almost as though he would look for trouble and I would be bailing him out. I took a backward step after that.

Another fight did me a favour when I was about fourteen I think. It was my inability to keep my mouth shut that got me into a "See you on the field in two minutes then" moment, and the corridor was going one way with people rushing to the field to see Harry getting his ass kicked by a year above lad who was known to be handy. I couldn't back out, I wouldn't be able to show my face if I did, I had to just face it and do the best I could. We faced each other, the crowd baying and chanting, "Fight, fight, fight, fight, fight". Of course in those days we were still gentlemen and the worst you could expect is a fist coming your way. The cowards nowadays hunt in packs and carry knives to get the first jab in as a surprise. Utter cowards who wouldn't have stood a chance in the 80s and 90s with just their fists to sort their disputes out.

After some tribal footwork it became a bit of a wrestling melee where somehow he ended up falling over on top of me so his jaw collided with my shoulder. He made his excuses and left much to my delight. I couldn't understand the reason for his swift exit but all was to become clear when I heard he had gone to hospital with a broken jaw and the word was out, "Tangye broke Mark's jaw in a fight on the field". I didn't deserve this reputation but I wasn't going to complain and was willing to take the kudos which helped me avoid several fights in the future I am sure. I have met Mark since and we are able to laugh over the whole incident!

I have worked single-crewed for much of my career mainly through being a Sergeant and being in Firearms often meant I got sent to an incident by the Control Room because it was assumed I'd be okay and would be able to sort it. I would say that being brave was overcoming a fear to achieve something. You won't get me potholing any time soon, and if I did that would be brave. When I see the confined spaces people get through it just fills me with terror. It's something I could imagine panicking over and becoming useless to all around me. So maybe that makes me not brave at all. Was it brave to tackle the cash-in-transit robbers? I think not, because I found it fun quite frankly and I found it outrageous that someone should think they could attack someone going about their normal business. It was almost selfish of me!

I received a Judges Commendation in 2019 for an occasion when I was team leader on containment where a man had threatened his wife in the street with a knife to her throat having dragged her out of her car. He had run into their house because fortunately she was able to lock herself back in the car when a neighbour came out to intervene. In pure medieval style he heated cooking oil in a wok, added sugar and washing liquid to it to make some sort of napalm and threatened to throw it from the top floor window to hit officers on the containment outside. We turned the gas tap off outside the front of the house which sorted that little issue out! He told us he had put newspaper down his shirt to absorb any Baton gun round or Taser and a cushion down his groin to prevent the same. He cellophaned two huge kitchen knives to his hands threatening to stab any officer who approached him.

As the only threat was to himself, time was on our hands and the negotiators seemed to be making progress with him. Without warning however he appeared in the garage having come through from the back garden. With knives raised and shouting, he walked towards me out of the front of the garage, I shouted at him to put the knives down which I am sure woke the rest of the containment as we had been there for several hours with not a lot happening. I approached him and at the point I knew he wasn't going to pay attention to a word I said, I Baton gunned him, aimed slightly higher than I would normally due to the cushion in his trousers. The round hitting him square in the chest. I shouted, "Loading, loading, loading", flipping the lever to open the breach, grab the back of the Baton round case, flicking it out over my right shoulder and immediately reaching for my spare round slotting it into the breach, slamming it closed and back on aim. He had buckled over but regained his composure as I reloaded and he was reaching up to close the garage door when my colleague came forward with a Taser and fired... having little effect due to the padding but another officer fired their Taser and he fell like a abandoned cooling tower that had just been dynamited, his knives still strapped to his hands.

I should remind the reader each officer had a Glock pistol loaded with a spare magazine on them, along with a G36 carbine semi-automatic machine gun for want of a better description, and yet this man who turned out to be high on drugs, extremely violent and determined to kill a police officer was dealt with in a fashion that caused a small red mark in the middle of his chest which would have smarted somewhat the next day but at least he was alive to feel it.

I was extremely surprised to hear of a Judges Commendation for the officers involved. All was on Body Worn video and it looked quite impressive on film however nothing too extraordinary. There was nothing we did that was different from training and even though looked quite dangerous I suppose, nothing too dangerous because of the training and teamwork we relied upon so much, but let's say I wasn't going to turn the Commendation down. After all, apart from my Cash-in-Transit Commanders commendation this was my only other one in 30 years of front-line policing which made me feel a little bit rubbish to be honest! I say this in jest, it is known that you have to rely on your supervisors to put you forward for recognition and as a Sergeant, your supervisor is hardly ever present, especially on Firearms so is rarely aware of particular circumstances of note. I am always present with my officers during the shifts so have regularly put my officers or others forward for recognition. Any awards are nice to show the grand children eventually I guess when they only see you as a blubbering idiot moaning "I used to be someone once!"

I look at bravery belonging to those who felt it was highly likely they were either going to die or be seriously injured. Those soldiers who put themselves forward to protect their colleagues, that's true bravery. I don't feel doing something that statistically shows you will make it through without a graze is bravery. I

197

confidently march into a hostile environment because I know the chances are I will be fine and if I am not, I'll probably live.

You could also ask whether alcohol makes you brave. Probably foolish, as you are no longer weighing up the odds of success which is what you do when deciding on a course of action. Does the potential success outweigh the risk? I was in Dublin on a stag-do with 10 military personnel from Culdrose. They were all Navy guys and we were all staying in a hostel that looked as though it was designed by EasyJet due to the hangover unfriendly bright orange colour scheme on the walls but it was cheap! Having sat next to a guy on the plane on the way over I was quite humbled with what he had gone through. Having chatted for a while I discovered he was the pilot of a Merlin Helicopter which had gone out of control heading for the Atlantic Ocean at a steep incline when he explained, "You are meant to get into a crash position but this was not survivable at that speed and angle so I just decided to chill and await the end". The helicopter went into the water, the windscreen held and he resurfaced.

Being a Navy pilot he said, "And do you know the most indignant part of it all?"

"No?" I replied, hanging onto every word...

"Being rescued by the bloody RAF in a Sea King", he replied with a cheesy grin across his face! "I nearly turned them away and they never let me forget who rescued me all the way to the hospital!"

It was at the time the smoking in public places ban was on in Ireland and we loved it, having woken up not feeling as though something had wire-brushed our throats and smelling like we could go out in our same clothes we had worn the night before.

On the second night, I got separated and was wandering around the streets of Dublin attempting to get some sort of navigation going with landmarks I thought I recognised but probably didn't. I was, shall I say, a little inebriated having supported the local community by consuming enough Guinness to give the brewery workers a day off. I was crossing a rather quiet road to get to the pavement on the other side when I was approached by a shadowy figure who immediately demanded money from me.

I was a little startled by this at first, but then quickly sobered up enough to think... 'Shit, if I punch him, I'm a drunk cop in Ireland and this could end my career". This was my genuine first concern. I dismissed the fact I could be stabbed by what I could now see was possibly a knife in his hand. I knew justice was never as good as it could be and being a police officer was not going to help you at all if you were drunk at the time of the incident. It was likely the chances CCTV hadn't picked up the lead up to the incident or a passerby would report they just saw the copper punch the nice man standing there. Okay, unlikely but enough of a concern which diminished enough for me to see him flying back onto the pavement with the silver flash of steel spinning off across the pavement. I had punched him in the chest as hard as I could because it would mean less or no blood and if a complaint was made it wasn't so damning.

As I slowly sauntered off in a random direction I casually looked back to where the incident had taken place to see my attacker lying on his chest whilst reaching far underneath a parked car attempting to recover his knife. I remember sniggering and saying under my breath, "Man, you're a shit robber!"

Somehow I was teleported into my bed and I woke up feeling a little jaded reaching for the sunglasses to combat some of the orange. I was listening to everyone's tales and adventures, scanning the couple of empty beds and trying to put together the evidence to show where they could possibly be now. It was about 3 hours after I had potentially been the victim of a robbery. Another chuckle and I put it to bed. I think it's because the attempt was so rubbish and the alcohol thinned out the potential threat to me, I didn't feel any trauma from it in the slightest.

This is why I am so supportive for children and teenagers to get into some sort of contact sport such as martial arts, rugby or boxing because if a person who hasn't experienced a contact sport is slapped in the face they often go into freeze mode, completely shocked and traumatised. If they are used to the occasional slap, then they often go into fight or flight mode. I attended a stalking in Exeter where a 15 year old girl realised she was being followed at night whilst she made her way home. The man ran up to her from behind and grabbed her. She screamed and kicked out before running. 10 years of karate had taught her to do that.

She didn't need to use the karate skills to stick him on his back-side, she simply needed to use the confidence to react to a dangerous situation the way she did. It probably saved her from being raped and that makes 10 years of attending that club worth every minute.

21. The Gravel Driveway

It was quite early in my career and I was often single-crewed going about my everyday patrols. Mainly attending burglaries from businesses overnight where drug addicts had been breaking into barber shops and estate agents after their £50 float and coffee funds. I used to take an Argos brochure around with me so distraught house burglary victims could point out the type of stone in their necklace or nearest ring to the one stolen from them. Time seems to have moved a lot of crime online now as there don't seem to be the burglaries anymore. Expensive jewellery doesn't seem to be so popular either with just as bright cheaper jewellery being available. It's far easier to carry out a fraud online than it is a burglary anyway.

Then there were the "Concern for Welfare" calls. Those elderly people who hadn't been seen for a few days or god forbid weeks, particularly bad in the summer months when things, i.e. bodies tended to turn to treacle and seep through the ceiling of the flat below. I have no idea why when searching a flat or house for a body, the bathroom was always the worst, which is why I'd open each door very slowly indeed as if something was going to jump out on me! The call always came in at night and for some reason there was often a gravel driveway involved. It was always a dark night too, and I knew I could never ask for assistance because why would I need someone to accompany me but to hold my hand so I knew I had to just face my childish fears and get on with it.

I remember a call with just those circumstances involving a concern for welfare of an elderly man who lived alone in a large house. I made my way to the large detached Victorian house in need of a lot of repair. Think of a Scooby Doo house and you are pretty much there and you may as well include the bats flitting around the chimney for good measure... with the moonlight just enough to form long creepy shadows from the trees that surrounded the property. I stopped the car in the driveway and paused looking at the scene of hell in front of me. A gent in his mid-eighties and he's not been seen for 4 days. He lives alone and the post is building behind the front door. Not a light on in the house I note, as I step out of the car leaving my cap on the back seat. No need for ceremonies here.

I can just about see my frosty breath billowing out in front of me against the moonlight and feel the hairs stand up on the back of my neck and then rush down my arms, every hair on high alert for danger. I was very unhappy but knew there was no choice. I had to save my face in front of my colleagues who no doubt were all slightly relieved it wasn't them who had been sent. I step forward towards the huge foreboding cliff of a house towering in front of me like a north Cornish cliff. No doubt a place of splendour in its hay-day but had long lost its polish and pristine paintwork. I wonder if the gent who owned it now had moved in with his wife one exciting day in the 60s and maybe things just hadn't been quite as fruitful as they had hoped. Maybe she'd died leaving him in this huge unwieldy house, just him without the skills, energy or finances to keep on top of the bills.

As I am musing over this I feel and hear the crunching of the gravel under my feet as I make my way towards the front door. I switch on my 6 cell Maglite torch and for such a large torch see its pathetic attempt to throw out a 3 candlepower light, just about reaching the ground in front of me. I have been meaning to buy some more batteries for a little while as the station battery supply runs out as soon as they are replenished. I step up to the large worn wooden front door and with a false optimism, press the doorbell and wait. No response as I had expected but I did hope for some signs of life. I push the door but there is no give. You never want to be the copper who smashed an expensive window when the door was open all the time, it's happened too many times before. I decide to walk around to the left side of the building to see what options there are. The whole place seems shut off to the outside. No signs of life at all and so I'm now glancing at the windows, looking for a single glazed small window to smash where I can reach in and open a larger one below to let myself in. I can see what looks like a basement arched window appearing as if from out of the ground. As I move closer I see there are steps that lead down to the base of this window and a window which shouldn't be too expensive to replace; I can get through it once broken.

I shout the gentleman's name. "Mr Brown!" Nothing.

"It's the Police!" Still nothing.

I pull my truncheon out of my pocket that runs down my trouser leg and put the strap around my wrist. I aim for the corner of the window and line the tip of the truncheon up. A quick pause, a last chance for someone to shout and then I give the window a sharp tap. It immediately cracks across the whole diagonal and another tap causes a large shard to drop to the ground creating a loud smash I thought would wake the whole neighbourhood. I carefully put my hand through the triangular hole and turn the latch letting it swing open towards me. I forlornly shine my useless torch through the window into the gloom of the room hardly casting a glow. It's no good, I'm going to have to climb into the unknown.

Right foot in then my left and into the room I drop feeling what's under my feet, a musty smell filling my nostrils. I feel newspaper I think, but it's so dark I cannot see what I am walking through, putting my arms out in front of me as I begin to traverse the room to warn me of anything ahead. My fingers make contact with a wall and I feel around for the door frame. There has to be a light switch and after a bit of feeling around I click the switch and the room is thrown into a flood of light. Brilliant, my first light for some time and I suddenly feel very safe.

It quickly dawns on me I've just lit what I have already crawled through but am yet to light what is in front and I realise that every light switch is going to be the far side of what I want lit! I see the worn wooden stairs with stripped paint leading up from this basement stretching up ahead of me. I shout again, "Mr Brown!" Still nothing so I begin climbing the stairs feeling with my hands either side of the narrow stairway running up the uneven walls, the light giving up its effort to follow me.

I am now levelling out onto the ground floor and can see the dim moonlight some distance off coming through the front door glass panel. I decide to go towards it to open it, somehow feeling as though I am letting in some security and safety. As I make my way towards the door I hear a whimper and swing around to my right to the doorway of a lounge area and I immediately see two very shiny eyes looking up at me from the ground. I immediately flick the light switch on in the room and our gazes fall on each other. I was looking at an elderly man's face with the immediate expression of utter relief. A face that had thought all was lost, someone who had given up on ever being rescued.

"Mr Brown?" as if it would be anyone else.

He nodded with a break of a faint smile. His grey haggard growth of beard gave the length of time away but how had he survived so long? He pointed at some bottles of Corona lemonade next to his bed. He'd made his base in the lounge to cut down on heating and the necessity of climbing the stairs and he clearly had a liking of lemonade which he kept next to his bed. This had saved his life when he'd stood on a stool to pin up a draft excluder curtain over the doorway and had unfortunately slipped off, falling to the ground. He had quenched his thirst over time by reaching for the lifesaving lemonade just within arm's length whilst unable to regain his feet. He was usually clean shaven and he now had a substantial growth going on. It was with great relief I radioed the control room for an ambulance which I knew would attract the interest of other units around for a good job well done. I have no idea what happened to that old gentleman after that but I know as a young police officer I did my bit. It taught me there was nothing to fear but everything to gain with these incidents. So often the more likely you felt they were going to be dead, the less likely they actually were.

22. VIP Protection

I had the utmost privilege of being a member of the VIP Protection Team (Prot) for over 15 years. I have stood next to Her Majesty Queen Elizabeth on 5 separate occasions, I have worked with all the Royals numerous times, and a large number of political leaders both national and international. I haven't tweeted on any of these for very obvious reasons. I have even had coffee with Obama when I thought I had been given a rather low-key head of state to look after at Nato in Wales. We were trying to make good speed on foot with our principal in the conference centre and I was leading the way. Suddenly David Cameron and Obama blocked our way and Obama's Secret Service asked if we could wait for a moment so myself and my party including my VIP had to remain in their tight circle for some 5 to 10 minutes whilst they chatted over coffee.

The Americans look and sound American, it sounds obvious but they have this aura about them. I love them, believe me. They are passionate and they are proud, all things the British are too embarrassed to be. My colleague Richard Hughes, another Devon and Cornwall VIP Officer seconded to Nato, was looking after the convoy of Obama whilst he was at the airport. He had watched Air Force One arrive and having seen the presidential convoy on standby for some time, sauntered over to one of the Secret Service guys standing to attention at the front. "So..." he enquires, trying to make conversation and feeling slightly awkward. "What's it like working with the President?"

I know, I'd have been embarrassed at that question too, but the answer was immediate, loud and curt.

"It's an honour to work for the President, Sir!"

This is where I should be able to put a shocked big-eyed and stunned emoji because that was what his face was. "Right... right, thank you... bye then!"

Richard slid away silently realising the Americans were really quite different from us British protection officers. I can understand it as they have quite a bad history of losing presidents or at least getting them shot. They therefore eliminate threat whereas we in the UK reduce the threat level to a proportionate and manageable level.

I have been fortunate to drive a backup car with Met outrider motorcycles through the City of London at night with sirens and blue lights through Trafalgar Square to The London Marriott five star hotel where I had silver service breakfast the following day, before taking the Head of Nato to Number 10 the following morning. I have attended Buckingham Palace on more than a few occasions and sampled its excellent coffee and tea, and attended Windsor to see the Queen inspecting her horses gifted to her by the King of Bahrain. There have been many times I have thought, "Well, that's something to tell the grandkids" and it's one of the reasons I thought I would write this book. To be honest, if it is just read by my children and maybe eventually the children they have, then that would be nice. There is then a permanent record of some of the experiences I have had just as my father did with

'Facing the Sea' by William Kimber publishers. If someone decides to publish it, then that would be very flattering but I'm certainly not doing it for that.

Devon and Cornwall had just under 3000 uniformed officers and of those 120 or so officers were Armed Response officers of which I was one. Of those approximately 14 or so were VIP protection officers. Devon and Cornwall received between 50 and 60 Royal visits per year. These would be ceremonial occasions such as the Queen decommissioning HMS Ocean in Plymouth, visits to several local businesses employing local people celebrating a special occasion and of course many charities celebrating occasions too. Several times a year we are required to go to London where they were running a conference such as the Commonwealth Conference or the Anti-Corruption Conference at which the Nigerians stayed in £5000 a night hotels. They hadn't quite got the idea! I am quite used to the secondments now and it's very familiar to me. It's always a great surprise to know who you have to look after for the week. I would be issued with a brand new Range Rover with approximately 200 miles on the clock, a credit card and of course I would have my Glock pistol in my covert holster under my suit jacket. Okay, there was a slight feeling of James Bond about it all which was highlighted to me when I was walking through the City of London just as the homeless were starting to come out and make their beds on the pavements. It was clearly a time which I felt was theirs and their time I was interfering with. I was on my phone to my wife at the time and apologised for cutting her short saying, "Sorry love, my phone is shining out like a belisha beacon. I think I'll have to put it away and call you back later".

I thought for a moment feeling that slight bulge of Glock 17 with magazine inserted with a spare magazine on my hip and said, "No, don't worry love, I think I'll be just fine, what were you saying again?"

I will not go to London without fulfilling my main mission of course. My late Father, a Spitfire pilot, had a favourite shop that being Fortnum and Masons and when I visited this shop I immediately saw why. As you walk into the grandness of displays before you, it has the aura of splendour and richness, yet has the atmosphere of being welcoming to all. I didn't feel out of place at all. It has style and professionalism but warmth. I could immediately see why my father loved this place. I now ensure I buy my tea from there; it has to be Fortnum and Mason's loose tea of course, and it has to be Countess Grey. It completely hits the spot with a subtle taste of Earl Grey and a citrus zing.

No one was more surprised to have been asked whether I would apply for the VIP course. I assumed the instructors may think I was a bit too lively for the subtleties of VIP. I mean I knew I was keen to have a happy and jovial ARV Section who wanted to come to work because it was fun, but they knew that when we had to be professional then I absolutely insisted on it. The job always came first and thank goodness this part of my character bled through to the instructors.

I would love to give you all the gossip but I may disappear overnight if I did, but I can certainly tell you a few things that did happen. There is a lot to talk about after 15 years! The role did involve a lot of planning, including attending recce's at the venues and if it involved two VIPs over two counties, who used trains, cars and helicopters this could be quite a logistical exercise. It meant meeting and working with many interesting people and visiting some fascinating places. I can say I see how they work. I see how the Princess Royal attends all the charities being thoroughly knowledgeable on the subjects. I see how she genuinely cares deeply about such charities for the homeless for example, and how she can share information and contacts from one to the other to boost their fundraising capabilities. I see how the Prince of Wales works relentlessly late at night, night after night. How he again deeply cares and how he stopped our convoy in a country lane to accept a bunch of flowers from an elderly lady waiting outside her cottage. No cameras, no people, just her and a few startled protection officers jumping out of our cars wondering what was happening, but it made her day when he shared a few words with her. No one will believe her of course! I see Prince Edward talking to school students about the Duke of Edinburgh Award, something I have been involved with for the past 35 years, and I see the effort he makes to put fun into the day for them, and he succeeds. Again, no media attention necessarily, just him making all those students feel special, feel as though they have achieved something and generally have a good day. And then there is the more mischievous Royal who has been known to cause a stir or two, but that's where I stop although you can no doubt guess who that may be! And now of course, things have developed since writing that paragraph!

I was having coffee with my good friend Jon Goodman at the Atlantic Hotel in Newquay recently. I'd had a wonderful walk at low tide from Lusty Glaze Beach to the harbour with my terrier dog Arthur. I had texted Jon to see if he was available and indeed he was himself out and about at Little Fistral just off the headland. Having met up, we were chatting about how time had gone so fast since our junior school days at Edgecumbe School. I had just reached my 50th Birthday! Jon suffers badly from epilepsy which has been incredibly debilitating for him but he has managed to be the number one force for good in Newquay creating numerous charity ideas and improving the town in numerous ways including setting up a local DIY SOS where he gets local businesses to contribute to community projects. He begins to tell me the story when his daughter Jessica and he were in Truro and he saw a cavalcade arrive just outside the Town Hall and the doors of the limousines swung open where men in sharp suits exited and stood to attention surveying the crowd around them. I was part of the team taking Prince Edward to a venue there and local police were also on hand to assist with traffic.

Jon is chuckling as he recalls this story, taking a swig of coffee as he starts telling it with a beaming smile. He goes on, he was moving to the front of the inquisitive crowd to see who the visitor was, pulling his teenage daughter through with him. He exclaims, "It's Edward!" and his daughter gives a rather uninterested expression in response. There's a slight pause as he sees HRH shake some hands and walk into the main entrance of the Town Hall, and then Jon scans the protection officers following him in and he sees me.

"Oh my God!" he screams, "It's Harry!"

At this point, Jessica's jaw drops and she pushes her elbows out to get a better look, lifting herself up onto tiptoe. She has a huge beaming smile on her face and her eyes are dancing around the streets looking for... Prince Harry! "Where... where is he Dad?!" she impatiently stammers, "I can't see him".

"There!" replies Jon, "it's my mate Harry... Harry Tangye"

Jon chuckles and almost snorts his coffee through his nostrils as he brings this story to an end... "Mate, no offence right, but to say she was disappointed is the understatement of the year!" This giant of a man is belly-laughing as he tries to steady his coffee on his lap! He's a good man is John. There should be more like him. He's already attracted many local awards for his volunteer services to the community. He's attended a Royal Garden Party for his efforts and it will be a tragedy if he doesn't have a bigger title soon. We need more people like him.

I was assisting looking after a politician whilst they were on holiday in Cornwall. It was a big one and I don't wish to give too much away but they attend there regularly! They had decided they wanted to try some kayaking and the Met officers were a little nervous as they hadn't done much kayaking being more city people so they were very pleased when I said I would tail the VIP as I had been brought up on Cornish Beaches and was very familiar with the sport. I would be a shadow so to speak, not interfering with him or his family's experience but I would be able to radio the current locations as we progress down this very large river several miles long and a mile wide in areas.

It was a couple of hours into this trip and all was going well. The Met crew were happy as they could see the progress from my reports. I was lazily paddling with no issues and I was marvelling on how wonderful it was that I was being paid to do this. It was when we turned a large right-hand bend and the water became a little more choppy that I realised I was taking on water. I could feel something was wrong at first. Either I was getting very tired, or the kayak felt a lot heavier than it had felt earlier. I quickly radioed my predicament to base camp and told them I would be fine making it to shore, but my VIP who no one had a clue was on the water, would be carrying on without me. No one knew he was there of course so he was quite safe, hiding in plain sight so to speak. I would empty the kayak out on shore and I felt sure I could catch him up again.

Everyone was relaxed. I wasn't that far from land and I managed to paddle there in 5 minutes or so. I was quite surprised by the weight of the kayak and it took some time to turn it upside down and pour the water out of the drain hole. Once empty I looked for any obvious cracks or splits but there were none. I calculated that at this rate of leakage I would have an hour and a half of floating time left, and my paddle would be over in only an hour or so looking at how far

215

we had already been. I had a life preserver on over my Quiksilver shirt, I wore shorts and sandals with my police radio in my top pocket in a plastic bag. I threw the empty Kayak into the water and jumped onto it, spinning my paddles like a paddle steamer making its way across the ocean and I made very good progress towards the dots in the distance.

I could see my VIP as they were making their way across the estuary. I doubt they had even turned around to see my issues as they were too busy having their own fun. It was about 20 minutes later when I had that sinking feeling again and it was happening fast. The kayak was slopping from one side and as I pulled the opposite paddle the body of the kayak threw itself onto the other side. A small panic began to manifest itself. I gazed across the estuary and saw my target, a slipway leading from the beach to a yacht club. I was heading for that but I couldn't risk grabbing my radio, I needed every second to get myself over to that beach and it was still 300 metres away. There were a large number of yachts moored between me and my goal, and I would have to weave myself through them too before I reached sanctuary.

I was now just 100 metres away from dry land when with one more death throw of a paddle the kayak flipped over onto its back like a surfacing whale throwing me unceremoniously into the freezing water. My first reaction was to grab the radio from my pocket which will have been submerged but may still be okay and press the transmit button to dramatically report my "Mayday, mayday" but to no avail. The radio was dead.

I pulled the top half of my body up onto my upside-down half-submerged kayak and began kicking my sandals as if they were flippers behind me. I made my way through the moored yachts trying to avoid eye contact with the disapproving skilled yachtsmen having their evening meal up on deck. One did ask if I was okay and I embarrassingly nodded and laughed a shameful snigger! If this sea could swallow me up.

I was trying to form a plan to warn the team. When the VIP turned up without me they would think the worst especially as I had previously informed them of me emptying the kayak of water the first time. This could soon become an international embarrassment for my VIP. If I didn't get word to my colleagues soon, there would be air-sea rescue and lifeboats looking for this VIP's bodyguard, disaster! I needed to avoid this at all costs, but how?

I eventually grounded my upturned craft onto land and pulled my waterlogged body from the ripples I'm sure were chuckling at me up the shingle. I tried to drag the concrete-weighted kayak up the bank but it wouldn't budge. It was going no further. For all intents and purposes I was dressed for a casual walk through the rather up-market town I had grounded myself on, but for the fact I was wringing wet. I decided to make for the yacht club to borrow a phone. I wasn't sure who I was going to ring as I didn't have any contact numbers on me, I didn't even know the log number for the job I was on as it's generically given and rarely used by us on plot. My police radio was dead and I had no other information at all. What the hell was I going to do?

I made my way up the slipway ignoring the sniggers from observers who had enjoyed the fact I had brightened up their otherwise eventless afternoon and approached the front door of the club with some trepidation. I realised there was no saving face here, I just had to go in and say it as it was, minus the fact I'd lost my VIP of course. I may just leave that bit out.

As I opened the door it immediately became clear there was an event happening there. This couldn't be worse. I had an audience and quite a posh one at that. I looked straight ahead, pulled my shoulders back and pushed my chest out. With sea water pouring out of my clothing I confidently strode straight through the birthday bash or whatever it was, and made my way up to the bar where I got the eye of the barman and clearly, distinctly and with full confidence announced, "I say, I seem to have sunk. Would you be so good as to lend me your phone please?"

The barman looked me up and down not quite believing what was before him, stretching his arm out with the phone in his hand, his mouth open saying absolutely nothing.

30 minutes later, having phoned 101 and got the FIM to call me back, I was rolling up to the VIP venue much to the relief of my colleagues and my to my utter embarrassment of course taking on much micky-taking including from the VIP I might add who insisted on calling me Bob for the rest of the evening!

There is never a dull moment in this job!

23. Ingredients to Make a Police Officer

Experience is everything, but you can blag it up to a certain point if you follow some basic pieces of advice. Knowledge is power, we know that, but it's tricky learning knowledge and takes a lot of hard work and time and is the knowledge you are learning in fact correct or learned from some academic without comparing it to practical everyday life. In other words, does it work in practice? and just to complicate this whole thing even more, in order to achieve knowledge and put it into practice successfully you could really do with some experience!

What really is a necessity is motivation in my view. In order to have the will to succeed, do the right thing and to achieve a worthy result you must have motivation. If you have all of these then you will be lacking only one thing. Yes, I had to add one more thing I personally think is a must to get the upper hand in life. I taught it to my kids from when they were tiny and I encouraged it as much as I could. Confidence is by far more important than any exam and can be a life-saver.

On day one of independent patrol, when this spotty 21 year old was being sent to domestic disputes, I realised I needed a cover story. I've already talked about fibbing a bit saying I was going through a divorce and had children just to be able to achieve some credibility in the eyes of the subject I was trying to win around. It would amuse me to see this would never be taught in police training college as it would fall foul of the integrity bracket, but you could argue I lied to obtain a good result for everyone and no harm was done, quite the opposite in fact. A little like telling your kids that Father Christmas existed, right.

I would never be shy about asking questions or advice and this has held me in good stead my entire professional career. I am often out of the loop with regards to procedural administration where specialist subjects in policing are concerned. In other words, if I have to complete a remand file, because my role means I rarely have to complete one and even if I remembered how to do it from the last time it would have changed multiple times since.

There are numerous different procedures changing almost daily and if you are in a specialist department you can become deskilled in those areas. Some officers from outside the department confuse that for becoming deskilled generally but they clearly have no idea of what is required in a specialist department and the continual updated training that's necessary. My head is filled with Firearms Tactics for buildings using 1 person, 2 person, 3 and 4 person, emergency search, searches for trains, vehicle options, open ground, woodland and planes. It's full of Operational Firearms Commander tactics, pursuit tactics, VIP procedures etc and all things that other officers don't need to learn of course. That's besides the general law and government guidelines and procedures we have to update ourselves on regularly, which is so necessary.

Being in a position where I found myself arresting someone wanted on warrant for example, who better to ask than a young inexperienced officer just out of training what the latest procedure is. The surprise on their face when I ask them if they can help me, insisting I do it myself so I know in future and thanking them for their assistance goes a long way. Too many officers feel it is some form of weakness to admit to a lack of knowledge. They have a reputation of avoidance and therefore laziness.

I learned in the early days if you were dealing with a job on the street, that as long as you got yourself a bona fide name and address, if you missed something else then the situation was always recoverable. Too many times officers would become muddled or stressed wondering whether to arrest or not when the situation wasn't clear, although I have had a motto of "when in doubt, arrest" which has never let me down. If you have a hunch something is wrong it usually is and it usually takes a lot more effort to recover the situation rather than acting positively in the first place and if you are talking yourself out of arresting someone, it is usually for the wrong reasons which will come back and bite you later.

So now we move on to confidence. Yes that's the other main ingredient and it's tough to find it if you aren't fortunate to be born with it but you certainly can gain it with time. Experience does give you confidence, and I think you can be trained to give the appearance of confidence even perhaps when you don't necessarily feel it. There are several times I may not be confident at all, but boy can I give the appearance of being it. This is why my New Year's Resolution is the same one every year. 'To blag the next 40 years as I have the last!'. One day they will find me out, but I'm getting away with it so far.

I give a demonstration to either young officers or indeed my children as teenagers. I ask them to imagine they are a group on the street corner and I approach them as I have no option but to walk through them to get to where I want to go. I walk through them with my head held high, shoulders back with a purposeful stride, no eye contact but as if I'm interested in something in the middle distance. As I approach the group I glance at other middle distance areas and stride through with purpose. Depending on the audience or how old I am, I may try an "alright?" as I walk through giving no time for a reply. I'm through the other side. I then return with my head down, with occasional nervous glances at the group, I quickly correct my view back to my feet and hesitantly walk through avoiding any form of communication. I'm practically shuffling my feet. I stop and ask the group. "If you wanted to have some fun with me, which one would you pick on?"

I go on to explain the reason why they would pick on the nervous me, is because I've portrayed myself as an easy target. It would be easy for one of the crowd to throw out a, "What you looking at dick-head?" Whereas with the confident me, it puts the nervousness on the other foot. 'He looks confident, why does he look confident? Has he good reason to look confident? Is he a martial arts artist...? will he make me look a twat in front of my mates...? he's gone, I've missed my chance.'

Alternatively you can walk around the other way if there is one, but as a police officer you cannot do that. (Incidentally my son has been doing Taekwondo for 8 years and is black belt so he should be okay in most circumstances!) As a Sergeant, I have mostly been single-crewed whilst on patrol. The PC's tend to double-crew and as I have other managerial responsibilities, it's not a great idea to tie up a perfectly practical Police Constable by tying them to me. There is however no hesitation on sending me to any incident particularly a violent incident. At the end of the day policing can be dangerous and even if a good result is completely non-achievable, I can at least make some difference by keeping bystanders out of the way, reporting back and collecting evidence. In practice I have never had an issue with grabbing the assailants by the scruff of the neck and if I got the odd knock it wasn't going to kill me. I work in Devon remember and crime is lower so we still sort out many a fight involving fists whereas in other major cities it's often a knife so I would have to adjust my position there. I probably wouldn't be single-crewed so much there either. One particular incident when this all went a bit wrong was relatively recently. This is a direct lift of a statement I did at 4am after the incident. It gives you an idea of how things can quickly get out of hand.

PS 13908 TANGYE - Statement

I am a police sergeant in the Devon and Cornwall Constabulary currently stationed at Exeter Armed Response Unit at Middlemoor, Exeter. I was working a night shift single-crewed starting at 10.00pm on Saturday 22nd August 2015. I carry weapons within ######### in the vehicle and I carry a Taser along with pepper spray and other protection equipment. I have been in the police on front line duties working shifts for the past 25 years and I have been in the Armed Response unit for the past 17 years or so. I am an

223

Operations Firearms Commander, a Firearms Tactics Advisor, I am a pursuit tactics advisor, an advanced driver, a VIP protection officer and back up driver, I am a senior investigating officer of serious and fatal road traffic collisions.

At 12.40am on the morning of Sunday 23rd August 2015 I was single-crewed in Exeter when I received a call from control room asking me to attend the ########## where there was a disturbance reported. This was next to ####### or is part of the same premises.

I arrived at the location 20 minutes later and as I drove into the car park, everything seemed very quiet. I felt the incident that had been taking place had obviously finished but I could see some heads of some people over what looked like pallets towards a house. I drove around and asked some people whether there had been a disturbance. A young male in a dark T-Shirt and wavy hair told me there had been some trouble but it had all finished now. I glanced around noting that everyone seemed quite drunk but also quite relaxed and there didn't seem to be any issues. I went over to the front door and asked someone who seemed to be quite sober whether I could speak to the owner. This gentleman was tall, about 35 to 40 years old and 5'9" tall, of slim build. He may have been the DJ I understand later. He offered me into the house and said the owner was at the rear of the house.

I asked if they could be called or I could go in, just to make sure all was okay. He and some others stepped aside. There was a very drunk male quite near me slurring his speech. I cannot remember what he was saying but he drew attention to himself as the others seemed to be quiet and relaxed. I walked into the lounge area and spoke to a woman who identified herself to me as the tenant of the house. She was white European, about 5'9" tall, of slim build wearing a beige woollen top or dress. She had blonde hair and was in her 30's. She was quite well spoken and looked nervous. She said, "WELL SOME OF THE PEOPLE HERE WON'T LEAVE AND I WANT THEM TO." Her face looked strained and she looked very stressed.

I quietly asked her which ones she wanted to leave, and she replied, pointing at the drunk youth who had been drawing attention to himself and some others around him. 'THEY ARE THE ONES, I NEED THEM TO LEAVE' she said quietly.

With that, the drunk youth who I now know is called P######### dob ####### shouted in my face, "HEY COPPER, YOU ARE THE PRICK WITH THE WHITE HAT AREN'T YOU?". He was white European, He had a red T-Shirt and was of medium build with black wavy hair in his 20's.

I put my hands on each of his shoulders and turned him around so he was facing the door, and with both hands remaining there, walked him out saying, "AND YOU SIR, ARE NOW LEAVING".

As he got outside the others around him were also outside around the door so my plan was to remain at the door stopping anyone coming in until some back up had arrived. He remained outside for a few seconds and then obviously got a little courage in front of his friends and walked up to me and began continuing his aggressive manner. "YOU ARE THAT P##K WITH THE WHITE HAT AREN'T YOU, YOU F***ING C**T".

At this point I told him he had to leave, and I took hold of him and firmly told him, "THAT, YOUNG MAN IS ENOUGH OF THAT BEHAVIOUR, YOU NEED TO LEAVE NOW OR WHEN THE VAN ARRIVES HERE, YOU WILL BE THE FIRST TO BE ARRESTED FOR A PUBLIC ORDER OFFENCE"

I felt this was a reasonable appeal to him explaining the law and that it was not acceptable. I was using my officer's presence and communications skills as I felt it was clear that the more I allowed him to use this aggressive manner towards me, the more the others around him would gain confidence to join in. Some of the youths around him were indeed starting to join in, saying, "HE CAN'T DO THAT, DON'T LET HIM PUSH YOU AROUND."

I was using Section 3 of the criminal law Act which permits me to use such force as is reasonable in the circumstances in the prevention of crime, and indeed Common Law also. At this time I was using open hands, and then taking hold of him and very much guiding him away using primary control skills. No force was required but he then came back again and I had to repeat this which is when he grabbed hold of me with his hands and pulled me towards him calling me a 'F***ING C**T'. I grappled with him as he had progressed from using active resistance by pulling away, and pushing to using aggressive and assaultive resistance, by trying to pull me to the ground. I realised by now I was in trouble.

There were a lot of men, approximately 10, fuelled with alcohol and I realised for just a few times in my career that these people could, and knew, that they could do what they liked to me and I was unlikely to know who had done what. It was dark, and the ground was slippery with mud. I realised that rather him take me to the ground and me be defenceless, I would use my defensive and offensive skills by using a take down on him. He was strong and I tried to use a leg swipe to trip him up, but couldn't get my leg far enough around so I kicked him in the shin as a distraction and whilst he had me pinned close to him, the only manoeuvre I could use was to get my arm over his head and pull him over my hip by wrapping my arm around his neck.

He went over my hip and hit the ground and I was pulled on top of him. I tried to reach for my radio but I couldn't free my hand from trying to restrain him on the ground. He was shouting at me saying "I'M GOING TO F####ING KILL YOU" or words to that effect.

I was too busy expecting a kick from behind to my head as the crowd of about 10 youths were now shouting and trying to pull me away. I was in great fear for my safety at this stage and I was extremely relieved to find PC ##### the dog handler arrive and shout at the youths to get back. At this point, another youth who I now understand his name is L####, dob ###### clamped his body around the head of P### who I was trying to handcuff but he was obstructing me from

227

doing so saying to P#### 'DON'T WORRY MATE, I'M NOT GOING TO LEAVE YOU'

I repeatedly told L### he was obstructing a police officer in the lawful execution of his duty, but he continued, repeating he wasn't going to let go of him. This caused major problems to me and PC #### as we couldn't safely detain P### whilst L#### was stopping us by obstructing us.

Whilst this was going on, a very large man in build but quite short in height that I now know as S###### DOB #### was becoming more and more aggressive towards me shouting at the top of his voice, looking directly down at me and aggressively gesticulating to me, saying, "I'VE GOING TO F***ING DO YOUR FACE, LET HIM GO OR I'LL F**K YOUR FACE RIGHT UP" He repeated this numerous times and I really felt we were in problems as we were trying to prevent L#### and P#### from assaulting us or getting away, and fearing for the baying crowd behind us from assaulting us. I felt very vulnerable.

With the assistance of PC ###, I managed to get the handcuffs on P### but he was trying to bring his knees up to strike me, so he was still a handful. I constantly felt people grabbing me and trying to pull me away, and I was waiting for a kick to my head. I had my hand on my Taser in my pouch on several occasions but I knew that if I was to use it or threaten to use it, it could easily be taken off me and used against myself so I decided to risk not using it. The same went for my pepper spray which again I decided was not safe to use.

228

I was aware that an urgent assistance call had been put up. I did press my urgent assistance button but I was aware that I may not have pressed it long enough for it to activate. I later found it hadn't so I was pleased that PC ### had done so. My radio was hanging off my QRV vest, and my ear piece was hanging around me so I had little idea whether help was on the way. I was very grateful for PC ### being there to assist me.

At about 1.10am that day with other officers arriving to assist, I shouted to P#### that he was under arrest for assaulting police and to L#### that he was under arrest for obstructing police in the lawful execution of their duty. I cautioned them and P#### replied, "YOU F***ING DICK, I'M GOING TO FIND OUT WHERE YOU LIVE, I'M GOING TO BURN YOUR F***ING HOUSE DOWN YOU F***ING C**T". I informed them they were arrested in order to prevent any further injury to themselves or others.

Other units soon arrived and helped control people. In the aftermath with officers taking control of my prisoners, I found the large male S#### still shouting threats saying he was going to 'Do Me' so I informed him I was arresting him for Section 4 of the public order act. I cautioned him and informed him that I was arresting him to prevent any further injury to myself or another. He replied, "OK, OK". I then spent the next 10 minutes with him whilst other officers arrived to maintain some order. At this time he became very apologetic saying this wasn't necessary. I loosened his cuffs and double locked them to make them more comfortable for him as well as putting his hands in front of him.

A couple of minutes later, I informed them they were all arrested for Affray and that they were still under caution and the same conditions applied.

Even though I was not able to press my emergency urgent assistance button on my radio, I attempted to. I have only pressed this twice in my 25 year career. I felt this was a situation where myself and PC #### were likely to receive major injuries, and I was extremely grateful for other officers arrival. It was obvious there was no respect for the police at all, and it was obvious there was no hesitation of laying hands on and trying to free their colleague and to threaten and assault police officers. This, unfortunately seems to be more and more common.

My uniform is a mess! I have mud everywhere and have received some slight cuts to my shins and knees which will soon heal. I feel battered black and blue and will no doubt ache in the morning however have no significant injuries.

I am aware of at least two other males who were a constant threat to me and PC ####. They were threatening and trying to pull us off their friends. I cannot really describe these.

****
****

Mr S### and Mr P### were fined. Mr L### was given a conditional discharge. I attended court on 5 separate occasions which meant officers were brought in to cover my night shifts from their rest days. This is common and causes even more stress to resources.

24. This is What 140mph Looks Like!

Twitter has often caught me out and every time I think I have it sussed, it stands up and kicks me in the balls again. If I have a direct message on my Twitter account from a local paper journalist asking whether I would like to comment on a tweet I've recently done I immediately know it's going to get uncomfortable. The uncanny thing is that my wife never has a clue of the impending storm until she goes to work and her colleagues say, "I see your husband's in trouble again!"

I had put a couple of tweets out with short videos, one through some country lanes videoing as a passenger whilst my colleague drove the car expertly overtaking vehicles in front. I put another on the motorway whilst negotiating traffic whilst my colleague videoed it. I'm giving a commentary to explain my observations. This final of a series of 3 tweets showed what the top end speeds looked like when travelling with minimal traffic at night.

I carefully review the footage for anything someone could pick up on as, believe me, some people live their lives scanning tweets to cause problems for the author. I would not be surprised if I put a picture of a beach with the title, "Having a lovely day today" (I wouldn't as it's quite a dull tweet) someone would react with, "Well that's disgusting, you should be thinking of people with agoraphobia you should". Seriously, I have used the rolling eye emoji on many occasions when I am in fact trying to grab them by the neck and shout, "Why don't you just shut the f**k up and get yourself a life!"

Well, the proverbial hit the fan quite frankly with a large number of people especially on Facebook by all accounts, saying how terrible and dangerous it was for me to travel at those speeds. It rolled on and there were even discussions on local radio on the subject. I was doing some decorating at home for the weekend so I have to say I was pretty pleased not to be at work to receive any fall out. Hopefully by the time Monday came things will have calmed down a bit. There was also an awful lot of support and quite frankly I knew I hadn't done anything wrong. The complaints were from people who lived in a naive safe world who thought they knew what went on out there in the world but didn't in fact have a clue. I didn't speak to the media team at all about this, but decided to put this statement out when it didn't seem as though it was going to go away in a hurry.

Statement regarding 140mph Tweet

After the considerable interest shown on my tweet of driving at 140mph at night on a predominantly empty motorway to a break in progress, I would like to add that we as Advanced Drivers in the Traffic and the Armed Response units will always ensure that if we drive at speed, we do not take unnecessary risks. This may seem like an unnecessary speed to many, however officers undertake numerous extensive driving courses which are refreshed regularly in order to keep them to the highly trained standards required for the role they do.

I myself am an Advanced Police driver, a VIP driver and a Pursuit Tactics advisor. I was a Senior Investigating Officer for serious and fatal road traffic collisions for 15 years. I am a Tactical Pursuit and Containment qualified officer and have over 20 years' experience of driving on full front line shifts. The geography of our Force area means we have to cover vast distances and this is always judged against the potential risk to the persons calling for police assistance, and the other motorists we pass along with ourselves.

We can make up considerable time on empty motorways between locations. General guidance by our driver training department is to keep top speeds to no more than double the speed limit. I would say however, I do regret the tweet, as it does tend to glamorise speed which is inappropriate and unintentional. I try to mix my tweet content to be fun, humorous, create debate, and to show the public what our everyday work is. This means I hopefully have the public with me when I want to discuss the more educational and advisory aspects of policing. I thank those who have supported me on this issue.

PS Harry Tangye

I decided not to put that if you disagreed still and you were a plumber or plasterer, I would be more than happy to tell you how to carry out your work and give you advice on your particular trade after you've been doing it for 25 years, but thought I'd keep the moral high ground.

Then I heard that my Chief Inspector of Traffic was coming onto Radio Devon to discuss the tweet. This will be interesting! I sat and listened to the presenter introducing the topic and the phone-in began with mixed reviews. "Well there's no need for it, we have to conform to the speed limit so why not him?" I mean you couldn't make it up! The second caller spoke some sense about it probably not being the best tweet to put up but police were trained and skilled to do this driving and then Chief Inspector Leisk came on. Here we go, deep breath, was he going to hang me out to dry?

I could have hugged him. He explained how this is exactly what we did and we don't apologise for it. We have a job to do and he acknowledged that he knew me and felt that I myself probably could see it hadn't been the wisest decision to tweet it in that particular way. That man fully supported me and I won't forget that.

My best friend Olly Tayler QPM of 25 years and someone I'm incredibly indebted to.

One of the numerous courses I've done. Some more fun than others!

My latest Section. They are quite shy!

I call this my Westlife photo. It was an afterthought after some standard poses. It's cheesy but I like it and the original lives in my spare toilet. Pat and Dean have their faces uncovered. Photo by Chris Fishleigh.

I spoke at the 'Smile' conference in LA after winning the overall winner of Police Twitter. Here I met Chief of Long Beach Robert Luna and we swapped hats. Thank goodness I had this photo when I was stopped at LA Customs with an American cop cap in my case!

Things can get wet and dirty in Firearms!

25. Snitches get Stitches

There have been quite frankly numerous other tweets with similar reactions but I will spare you the majority of them here! What I have learned is you can't criticise anyone however awful they are. If it's a gang leader comparing their stress to the PTSD suffered by our soldiers abroad then don't call them animals. This particular ex-gang leader said in an interview, "When you push a broken glass bottle into someone's face, it gets to you, you know".

I put a tweet out saying, "and when we haven't kicked our armed forces in the teeth enough, we can compare their PTSD to these animals'.

People get very upset because some people including some police officers and "experts" in mental health think you shouldn't call gang leaders who groom young boys into their gang and rape their "new girlfriends" animals. They are humans who had a tough upbringing so we should try to understand them. Fair enough, try to understand them so you can stop them, not so you can empathise with them and give them excuses. Clearly there needs to be a long term solution to prevent young black men taking to the streets with knives stabbing each other in tit-for-tat attacks. That will include replacing what the Conservatives short-sightedly took away, such as their communities in the way of community centres, boxing clubs, cadet clubs and youth centres when the grants were slashed, oh and the police numbers of course. They took the community officers away who were expert in knowing the community and nipping problems in the bud at an early stage and they took the police away who would have investigated crime and caught the offenders and given some deterrent.

There was devastation as we now know, and only a few MP's couldn't realise this was going to happen. They were happy to reduce our security mainly as they were secure in their own houses of course. They wanted to save money by getting rid of cops which reduced our security as a whole by selling the equivalent of the locks to our houses and that's not very sensible. So then they made 'Stop Search' a dirty phrase not having a clue what they were talking about and listening to the wrong community spokespeople, jumping on the hip and trendy bandwagon of slagging off the police and saying we needed change. Well, they got that and a lot of young people died.

We clearly need the long term solution but we also need robust no nonsense policing and a judicial system that says this behaviour is not accepted and if you do it you will be severely punished. It will send a message to the community and it will remove those from it who cause the danger. It clearly needs a change of attitude from the community as well. A tradition of not telling the cops, "snitches get stitches" is a main reason why so many feel free to murder at will. It's going to take a

few brave souls as a group to say enough is enough or things won't change. What I do know is the government well and truly messed this up and it cost lives.

What this tweet also taught me, is when reading an interview and clicking the Twitter logo to produce a tweet with personal comment from the article it's best to check what photo is automatically placed on the tweet from the article you linked. You can imagine how I lay myself open by not seeing the automated photo was a side profile of a black man and with my comments regarding "These animals" I think I got away extremely lightly indeed. The lesson here is check, check and check again.

It constantly surprised and impressed me how my Chief Constable Shaun Sawyer and Deputy Chief Constable Paul Netherton continually supported me through my Twitter years when I was getting a thorough battering particularly in the early days. As I've already said, CC Shaun Sawyer would call me at home sometimes in the evening to see how I was coping. His name would come up on my mobile and when you've had a Tweet not go down so well it would often make my heart sink. This man is in charge of a 5000 employee company remember, and he was ringing me up at home after some controversy. I have the absolute utmost respect for that man. He is a real people person who puts the people in his police force before that of his career. A particularly courageous man who was often the first to lead with controversial discussion such as not being able to offer the service the public had previously come to expect since the government cuts. He was the first to say this publicly which was against the tide as the chief officer and government mood was to say police officers had to be more efficient with less.

As Assistant Chief Constable at the time, Paul Netherton raised the issue in a Tweet of how unacceptable it was to have nowhere else for a 16 year old girl in his cells because there was simply no mental health support bed for her in the country. It created a lot of attention in particular from the Mental Health partners. Paul Netherton is a man of similar ilk to Shaun Sawyer and they are two men I can say I completely owe my time on Twitter to so it's them you should blame! The fact that Paul Netherton was awarded an OBE is completely deserved. There is justice after all!

They both knew I was there to do good, to support police officers and the role they do, and to highlight to the public what the police actually did for them but every now and then things would go a little awry! I remember parking my car in the Police HQ car park where my ARV base was and catching the eye of my Inspector getting out of his car after a particularly difficult public reaction to a tweet I'd put out a day earlier. I expected him to walk over to me and give me a bit of a grilling but he smiled, shook his head and walked off to his office instead! I needed that, and I appreciated it!

26. Selfie on the Bridge

It's a pretty ordinary day. Warm, I'd say hot even, and life was generally good. It's August 2016 and there's a hold up on the M5 in Somerset, and the back of the queue is backing up into Devon. It's been a while now so I'd best take a look. Taking a wander up to Junction 27 on our border I wisely decide not to commit further North so I go on top of the bridge that looks over the motorway.

Looking North I see the whole North side is static, so much so there are people out of their cars talking as if in a car park on a relaxed August morning, which it was of course but the motorway would not have normally been the place for it. The Southbound was empty of traffic and people, not even tumbleweed rolling across the three lane patch of tarmac normally bringing the hordes of holiday traffic. All those screaming children shouting "Are we nearly there?", and "I want the toilet, Mummy" and the "You're going too fast, Bob, you have 3 points already" to "We have to give the dog a wee, Gerald, he's crossing his eyes again". No doubt if those conversations could be recorded, they would make an interesting story.

Looking at these cars on the Northbound I saw a car with the occupants walking a dog to the side of the hard shoulder. It reminded me of when I stopped a Vauxhall Vectra Estate which had been speeding. 2.4 children in the rear with a rather plain-looking wife with a blonde bob, in the front passenger seat looking disapprovingly at her husband whom I had just asked if he could come back to my police car. On issuing him a ticket for his

91mph in a 70mph limit, I carried out a PNC check to see if he was on the police database. I didn't expect him to be so as he looked just as drab as his 2.4 children, his blond bobbed wife and his golden retriever I'd just seen in the back of his Estate which has to be one of the dullest estates in the world.

The operator tells me in my ear piece, "Known to police", Okay, this will be interesting, and up it comes. Armed Robbery, served 10 years in prison which was unexpected to say the least. So I had to say something. "An interesting history, Sir" I enquire, hoping for a reply, which I got. "Yes, my wife doesn't know about that side of my life. I would rather put it behind me so would appreciate it if you could not mention it to her."

I watched him go back to his car, and I admired the man really. He's got into bad ways and he had worked himself out of it. He wanted a normal life and indeed he got one. I wonder if his 91mph was his little bit of rebellion, just aching to get out from his rather dull existence.

So back to the bridge, I understand it's another poor soul threatening to jump off the bridge over the motorway in Somerset and they have got negotiators speaking to her. I am concerned as some of those people I am hearing have been left in hot traffic for nearly 4 hours and they are backed up into our area; I knew I had to do something. I was arranging for highways to go up the opposing carriageway whilst ensuring it was clear of opposing traffic which was the important bit and I would ensure good communication with Avon and Somerset Police whilst we carried out this manoeuvre. Highways crews could then take down a barrier and we could start getting some traffic back down the correct carriageway. They could then follow a diversion to get past the obstruction and this would stop a lot of any further delay. Typically just as the phone calls have been made and things are just about to be put in operation we get the all clear.

Now I knew that it will take at least half an hour for any delay to clear from the first car in the queue to the final car that was queuing so I decided this would be an ideal opportunity to put out a tweet. I know the local online news and radio channels cover my tweets so I knew that even if people in the queue were not following me which was likely they wouldn't be, they may be looking at local news to see what the delay was and they would realise they would soon be on their way. I also knew this was a sensitive topic being a suicide threat so it had to be handled carefully.

I needed a photograph, because that's what catches attention. The traffic on one side and the no traffic on the other side was a catchy photograph, but it could be seen as a library picture so I needed to put myself in it but my photo could not be too jolly or too falsely sad or it would look as though I wasn't taking the subject seriously. I was also restricted to 140 characters so it couldn't be too long winded. After considerable thought I tweeted as follows:

'Sorry guys and girls, someone threatening to jump off bridge, but now off and traffic moving. Take time to clear'

I finished the shift and didn't look at Twitter for several hours. When I did look at Twitter, the whole world seemed to have caved in on me. The Daily Mail had plastered me and my tweet all over their online paper with the title, 'Traffic Cops Bizarre Selfie'. The main part of the article was more about people complaining about the delay and very little of me doing the tweet but it was creating a merry hell of discussion and newspapers were loving it. I wanted to dig a hole and bury myself in it. I had no idea how my bosses were going to take this but I knew it was unlikely they would be pleased with adverse publicity. It is after all, much easier to take the side of the complainer.

And then the head of Devon and Cornwall Professional standards Superintendent Brendan Brookshaw intervened publicly on twitter, and he's been my hero ever since. He wrote:

'Harry, the PSD view is that this was an excellent use of Social Media for public info. Keep up the good work. Bb'

Other forces then joined in, and some very high ranking officers agreeing with Superintendent Brookshaw and numerous tweets came in congratulating the Force Professional Standards department for supporting their officers against the media who were trying to make a story out of nothing. Devon and Cornwall was leading the way again, and it came from the top. Many other Forces would have cut the Twitter Account for being controversial and causing unnecessary issues for their media team. I felt extremely fortunate I was in the Force I was and certainly wasn't taking it for granted.

Of course I became known for Selfies after that, and bridges of course which I was more than happy to go along with. I didn't take too many other bridge photos but once you get known for something it's very difficult to shake it off and I did use it to my own advantage on more than one occasion! I prefer a photo to provide more for the imagination as they are so much more effective and attract more attention. Instead of showing a road traffic collision scene with a couple of damaged cars, it's so much more effective to take something from a different angle, such as ground level may be of an indicator lens on the tarmac with the background blurred but letting the imagination fill in the gaps. Far less for people to get upset about with comments such as, "I know you didn't show the number plate, but everyone knows I have a Silver Ford Focus and now it's not on my drive". I found I will attract complaints from everywhere and even though they may have no claim, it's best to avoid them if I can. I constantly apologise to my poor media unit who have to work so hard on some of the results of my tweets. I was once told tongue in cheek that if I continued the way I was, they would have to take on another couple of staff!

I attended a pub one evening with the report that some of its clientele were being targeted by someone with an air rifle. It had been going on for a couple of days having led to some rather serious injuries. Having tracked down a witness who pointed out to me the window he suspected to have seen the suspect in, I was able to arrest the male who lived there recovering the air rifle, I took a photograph of the side profile of the rifle and tweeted that someone had been arrested.

I was contacted by a supervisor explaining CID had been very upset the photo had been published as any good barrister could argue any further witness was tainted from giving a description of the rifle as I had published a photo of it. Witnesses or further victims were far more likely to come forward having seen my tweet than be tainted by it. Did CID feel the side profile was so identifiable, the witness was going to suddenly come forward and pick it out of a selection of 12 air rifles all pointing at them! We would never prove by the description of the air rifle that that was the one that had been used in the offence. They all look so similar. It would be forensics that would do that and only forensics, however it showed that some people refuse to see the good that can come of social media. They don't see the benefits and therefore damn it wherever they can. It's so short-sighted. The man was convicted with an imprisonment of several years.

I am so grateful to the present Corporate communications team. It's a case of always being a discussion as opposed to a ticking off when complaints are received and how we can prevent something going a bit awry in the future. The previous temporary media boss was someone who very much didn't want to think outside the box and was quite happy to settle for the status quo. I put a short video out on a very wet winter's night. I was standing on the hard shoulder with blue lights flashing behind, rain pouring down and I'm asking the public to 'Slow the hell down' as this was the 6th aquaplane I had attended that night. I received two complaints from people, one who believed I shouldn't be making videos but should be getting on with the job instead, and the other saying I wasn't being safe by standing on the side of the motorway at night in such poor weather.

A meeting was held with my Chief Inspector, and I awaited the media supervisor who eventually rather gleefully came sauntering into the room with his large file held in both hands to emphasise how exceptionally important he was. He sat down as if he were a headmaster coming to chastise a pupil, opened the file with great enthusiasm and began his list of complaints against me for a number of tweets that had raised complaints. Let's say having been argued successfully against all of them up to then, he'd left the motorway one for last.

I was ready for him and I gave him both barrels. "How about you concentrate on the 28, 998 positive views with no complaints or highly supportive comments and how about you leave the two complaints for me to sort out? I can tell them I was standing in front of a broken-down car in the hard shoulder, with lane one completely cordoned off by the Highways Agency, and that I was waiting for a recovery truck, and that as I am videoing in selfie mode, I can also see what's behind me on the screen and how about I tell them to keep their own fat noses out of my business because that motorway has been my playground for the last 30 years so stay the f**k out of it!".

He stared at me in some disbelief, slowly shut his file and looked at the Chief Inspector. "Er, right", said the Chief Inspector glancing at me and then him. "How about you go out on shift with Harry some time?"

248

I made damned sure it happened and spent the whole shift with him going to every immediate we attended driving with that car on two wheels and when he gripped the rail above the door as we entered a tight bend onto the motorway on slip I said nonchalantly "Well that ain't going to help you!". Those tyres were melting and the pinking from the overworked hot engine could be heard 20 metres away. He left me that shift and I never saw or heard from him again.

27. How to Stay Alive as a Police Officer

This isn't going to be a lesson in avoiding bullets, dodging cars driving at you, ducking fists flying towards you or finding some hard cover when the trouble really begins. All that you can learn from a good Clint Eastward film, (let's face it, was there ever a bad one?) and you could even get some slow motion skills from The Matrix perhaps, but none of that will probably work in reality.

What I'm talking about here is something I've learned mainly from my late father in dealing with stress, and some I have stumbled across myself. Firstly, without a shadow of doubt in my mind the most important aspect of working as a police officer is to remember the quality of life is the most important part of your life, and so many people get this bit wrong. What I mean by that is that it is so much easier to deal with the stresses of work without any repercussions of mental illness if you remember to enjoy life over money or you can just be damned miserable if you decide early on that career and money is everything. There are plenty of bored, miserable and some suicidal millionaires.

So many times I have been asked, "So when are you doing your Inspectors exam, Harry?" I was asked this a couple of times by a very respected and now a good friend Supt Tim Swarbrick. I would instantly reply, "I'm not, Sir. What other rank would give me a fast car and a gun to play with all day?" Delivered with a beaming smile quickly convinced him I had made the right decision. He could see I was happy doing what I was doing and specialising in the role of Firearms

Officer, and he knew of many others who had woefully dragged themselves round Head Quarters with a blue folder in hand wondering where all the fun had gone. Live for the moment and not for the future that may never come. Don't be reckless, but do what you enjoy and certainly do not go up the promotion ladder just because it's there. Having decided this so many years earlier I found my stress and guilt had quickly dissipated. I could remain as a Sergeant and concentrate on the role I was doing, get better at it and specialise sideways instead of moving up the promotion ladder and there's something quite satisfying in becoming one of the most qualified in your field receiving the respect from ranks many above your own.

Quality of life also goes into enjoying the simple things in life. There was nothing better for me than to walk across Dartmoor with my dog assisting a Cornish school with their Duke of Edinburgh Award Students which I've done for the past 35 years, firstly with Newquay Tretherras School and then recently with Truro School. I have outlived 3 previous dogs who had the benefit of seeing the beautiful scenery of Dartmoor and the mountains, valleys and lakes of Cumbria. To put my tent up in gale force winds, buckle down in it with my Terrier Arthur, or Polo before him, zipped in tired and softened from the pub some hours before, hearing the rain battering my shelter and the winds attempting to shock it into submission, there is nothing more comforting and cosy. Nothing so warm and snug, to listen to the elements doing their best and failing to get at the cocoon that is me and my dog within. I never sleep so well.

Whilst wild camping on Dartmoor having had a beer or two that evening, there can be a need for a call of nature at the most inconvenient time. Waking up feeling as snug as can be in my sleeping bag with a pressure on my bladder I can hold no more, I pull myself out of my bag and unzip my tent to face the bitterly cold night outside. Standing in a t-shirt, pants and bare feet in damp walking boots, I take a couple of paces away from the tent, Arthur following and standing next to me. We both start to pee, side by side like father and son, and I realise I have no need for a torch. It's 4am and the moor around me is lit up brightly and as I glance up into the sky my breath is taken away in a sudden gasp. The stars, the stars as I have never seen them are like the brightest of sequins streaming their bright white lights down to the earth below. The reason I am now seeing them so bright in a huge never ending black sky is because there was simply no light pollution from nearby towns and cities. This is one of the most stunningly beautiful sights I have ever seen, and one I always hope to see again but the requirement of a cloudless sky is imperative for not only to see the stars, but to stop any reflection of light bouncing off the clouds ruining the whole effect.

I often go back to Newquay to check up on my elderly mother who still lives at the top of Lusty Glaze Beach. I was a lifeguard on this beach when I was 17 years old and worked several seasons including as a deck chair and surfboard hirer at the age of 16 during those wonderful summer holidays. My commute was approximately 3 minutes on foot! Going back to Lusty Glaze now I love to wander down those concrete steps and bury my feet in the golden sand. Pick up a worn smooth pebble and throw it as far as I can towards the sea but see it skipping along the glistening sand made firm by the previous tide that's now sitting further towards the horizon some distance away.

Arthur, my Border Terrier Jack Russell cross will yelp with excitement as he gallops after it, scuffing the stone with his nose to declare he's found it but then carry on to other items of interest including the sun-baked skull of a herring gull that would now never give up its tale of woe. To stride down onto the great expanse of beach and spin around to view the soaring cliffs that surround me sucking in the fresh salty air into my lungs, is a feeling I will never get bored of. I approach the ripples that frolic onto the sand, having used their last energy from hundreds of miles into the North Atlantic, it reminds me of the many hours of fun I have had in those waves as a child, a teenager and as an adult. When I take in this atmosphere, the billowing clouds and the crisp blue fresh skies I realise how lucky I am and my batteries slowly recharge. It helps to pop into the wonderful restaurant and bar that once sold rubber dinghies and ice cream to have a coffee or a pint of Cornish Ale and to catch up on Twitter messages, write this book or simply just do nothing and Arthur gets spoilt by the staff with treats in there too so he's quite partial to going in as well!

I have been so fortunate to have a wingman for most of my career too, which has undoubtedly saved my sanity. One of those friends you can ring at 3am if you've broken down and know he'll come and get you without delay. A man who would tell you if you were being a prat and one who would support you when you've failed a course and you are at your lowest ebb. A man who rings you out of the blue and says, "I heard you went to that shit fatal, mate, how are you?" Someone I have got quite drunk with on several occasions to say the least, one I flew Merlin Helicopters with when his brother, who is also now a dear friend, James, was an instructor at Culdrose Navy Air base, someone I was strapped to as we got winched down onto a pitching lifeboat off the coast of Wales, ridden motorbikes together, driven 8 wheeled army trucks through mud with, someone that if either of us pressed the red button on the other, we would both go down! That dear, dear friend is Sgt Olly Tayler QPM. I personally thank you, Olly, for being there my friend.

I remember going out in Helston with Olly and his brother for a few beers and an Indian meal on one particular visit, probably to one of the many Air Days we attended. We were always a little nervous of declaring we were cops so Olly and I decided to adopt the ruse we were biscuit designers. Well, someone has to do it, right? We ended up in a rather empty bar with a pretty but bored girl behind the bar serving our drinks. She quickly asked what we did and Olly's brother James, now a Search and Rescue pilot in New Zealand, said, "I fly helicopters". She looked across to Olly and myself and repeated the question and we gave our answer, "We are biscuit designers". She looked a little bemused, glanced at James and then back to us and said, "So biscuit designing, really?" She was hooked and Olly and I became a double act bouncing off each other with an involved account of how we had

254

designed the centenary digestive, the problematic issues of the design melting into itself and guessing she was a rather earthy person, Olly came out with the fact we sent the equivalent of the biscuit crumb mountain to the starving children in Africa. I suggest to all young men out there trying to get a date, don't say you fly helicopters, say you design biscuits!

Hold in the back of your mind that if you died tomorrow, you'd be thought of for a week in high probability and then rarely thought of again so is it really worth getting so stressed you can't cope with things? When I find myself getting a little stressed I remind myself of this and immediately chill out. I will do what I can within the time and if I can't, then the answer is I wasn't able to. That's that.

Blogs

28. Break a Window or Stab a Police Dog. The law Says it's The Same - Well it did!

I wrote this blog to try to drum up support for who is now my good friend Dave Wardell who was trying to get the law changed with regards Service animals being treated as no more than damage to property when they were in fact assaulted whilst working for the services. I am so pleased to say that thanks to Dave, Finns Law is now a reality which means any offender found guilty can have the full weight of the law thrown at them for injuring a service animal or worse. This account was made up of several incidents I have witnessed, and I was very pleased to say it got a very positive reaction from dog handlers. That's all I cared about! I now consider Dave Wardell a true friend and often meet up with him. He is one of the most warm genuine people I know, and selfless to the core. The world is a better place with him and his dogs, and they have certainly put away more than their fair share of violent criminals with Finn his beloved dog who has now retired, and now with his current dogs Hero and Diesel. Dave is currently running a campaign called Finns Law Part 2 which pushes for heavier sentences for cruelty against any animal. It was with them in mind I wrote this blog.

Storm is a 3 year old German Shepherd Police dog, who his owner Jim adores. They have spent those 3 hard years nurturing each other through 13 initial weeks of hard training and numerous courses and training sessions since. They are always at each other's side, can wholeheartedly trust each other, and will gladly put themselves in harm's way to protect the other from evil. The bond is unequivocal.

It's a Saturday afternoon, and Jim is steering his Police Ford Focus Estate through the back streets towards the report of the burglary. It's been called in by a neighbour and it sounds like a good one. A man in his late teens has been seen dropping down from a flat roof at the rear of a rather affluent looking detached house which backs on to some fields. He's been seen running with a small clutch of items towards the hedge of the rear garden when the witness sensibly decides to give up the view in priority for phoning the police.

Storm is in the back of the Focus in his cage. A beautiful glossy chestnut perfect specimen of a German Shepherd. He's in his prime. He's spent years anticipating his master's driving, every swerve and tight turn, ensuring he leans heavily on the opposing foreleg to keep himself balanced. Jim knows his best friend is holding on for dear life so tries to drive more smoothly, more than impossible in these back alleyways. Blue lights on this sunny day, but no sirens as we don't want to alert the burglar to our imminent arrival, the pay back is the angry stares from the elderly couple walking on the side of the road who glance over to see which boy racer is disturbing their peace. "Ah those cops again, not like in our day dear", he mutters to his wife, "Where's their sirens then? We should complain".

His wife ignores him like she has for the past 45 years and continues walking with her stick and her arm linked to her husband, watching the rear of the police car disappear around the next corner, the blue light extinguishing any wish she has herself, to make a complaint.

Jim is nearing the scene now, and runs his checklist in his mind. Tracking equipment just where it should be and best have Storm's toy with me for when he finds the burglar, after all that's what he thinks he is looking for!

The car grinds to a halt slightly scuffing the curb on the alloy. He winces knowing that that one will show no doubt, and he will have to report it later. He's out of the car and the neighbour is immediately pacing towards him with an excited urgency on her face. The car rocks even with Jim out of it as Storm knows what's coming next. He delights in the hunt that is to follow, and he can't wait to get started. Jim fixes his harness and tracking lead, a sign to Storm he isn't going for a gentle stroll, but this is business. The information is gathered as to where the suspect was last seen and having updated the control room on the radio, Jim is off, being dragged by Storm through the rear privet hedge. A thorn catches Jim's hand and scratches a deep gouge. He curses and half-heartedly apologises to the smiling neighbour waving him off like a teenage son going off to college. Storm is pulling steadily at the lead, trying to drag him at a pace he would rather go if left to his own devices, but Jim knows he has to keep him at just the right pace. Fast enough to make ground but not too fast so he runs past the scent which may have turned direction.

It's only a matter of minutes before he sees a track leading from a main road to a ramshackle shed at the far side of the field he is now in. Between him and the shed Storm is lapping up the scent. He is transfixed on it and it is leading directly to it. He wonders if there is a getaway car parked there, or whether that is where he will find his quarry hiding. He has to hurry, radioing for backup as he nears. He can hear the Police helicopter in the far distance, the thumping of the rotor blades breaking through the pounding of his heart in his chest. His heart beating from not only the stress it's been under on the track, but also charged by the adrenaline preparing him for what they may face ahead.

Up to the corner of the shed and no car has left yet, so maybe there is none. Storm rounds the corner as Jim shortens the lead for more control, and he hears barking. Storm is telling him he has found his quarry and now wants his toy reward. He's bouncing off his front paws throwing his head forward with a full row of deadly sharp and powerful teeth in the fullest view Storm can parade to the terrified victim. It's quick but Storm has lunged forward, Jim's confused for a second as he's meant to stand his ground unless threatened, but then he sees the flash of a silver blade streaking across the darkened shade of the shed wall, a yelp but the fight Storm has started now continues relentlessly, growling with a fixed jaw clamped heavily and stubbornly onto the victims thigh, shaking his head like a terrier on a rag doll, but the blade rains down again and the cries from Storms victim and from Storm continue.

Jim's utter horror seeps to the surface and he's trying to pull his beloved friend to safety whilst kicking out at the assailant. The knife flashes across again, and catches Jim's hand, but he doesn't feel it, he knows that now he is fighting for not only his dog's life, but his own. He realises they are alone with a frenzied attacker who will do anything to get away from this situation. Jim now kicks hard between the legs of the offender and immediately the knife is flung to the side and the surrendered assailant shouts, "Alright, alright, no more".

He pulls Storm away in a standoff position and Storm shouts his displeasure at his quarry. Jim leaves the lead just a little longer than usual to ensure the burglar doesn't think of running, and maybe if there is another accidental nip, then so be it. Jim is angry, very angry, but he's proud of his little boy, his best friend and as the helicopter swings around at low level drowning out the sounds of the barking, Jim glances down the side of Storm and sees blood, then quickly up to his shoulder, blood, and then his head, blood, and it's too fresh, too much to be from the burglar, no, please let it not be, but it's dripping, and dripping fast. Jim shouts on the radio for a car fast, he needs to get help for his friend. Storm slumps to his haunches, and then he lays gently down on his side, he shouldn't do that, he should still be barking until called off, but he's lost interest. Jim glares at the burglar lying down leaning against the shed wall holding his wounds, shouting at him, "Move one inch and I will kill you myself"

Jim cradles his friend. He's just 3 years old not even half-way through his working life, so much time, so much effort, so much training, and so much love, so much care, so much trust, and loyalty. And then it's no more as Storm ebbs away. He's replaced by a calm and peaceful tranquillity, a peace that is still only in Jim's head as he is distracted for a second by the helicopter dipping its imaginary wing and swinging off to the side as if a gannet saying goodbye to a dying gull caught in a gale. He stands over Storm whose chest has stopped rising, and weeps, placing the toy next to his beloved friends head. "You caught him, Storm, you caught him, my friend".

Officers take away the burglar, but one remains putting a hand on the shoulder of Jim. He watches a broken window of the shed reflecting the light of the sun against the chrome name tag of Storm, and a cloud moves across the sun, snuffing the last sparkle from Storm.

29. A Quite Unusual Routine

I wanted to get this blog right. I wanted to show from a near exact account of a genuine incident that happened to me relatively recently, how sometimes there may not be happy endings, where officers can't always give the answers to people's problems and to highlight the woeful inadequacy of the mental health system as it stands at the time of writing.

The heater is on, that annoying hum where you adjust the compromise of noise to the correct delivery of heat, just enough to keep you warm but not too much to make you over sleepy. My Police partner Chris is the driver today. He and I haven't said anything for a couple of minutes as the fatigue is setting in quite strongly now at 5.30 on this otherwise relatively quiet end to the night shift. The dull glow from the Police dashboard display buttons illuminated, waiting to be pushed into life and throw their red and blue lights around the countryside surrounding the car. Every push means a new emergency, means someone is in need of help, and they hope it will come soon.

The radio in my ear piece disturbs the humming of fan and car engine, but it's got my full attention. Every message is like unwrapping a mystery present. Excitedly listening until the message is revealed and it's either a gift to be happy with, one to be a little nervous of, or one that could be thrown to the back and forgotten but you have to acknowledge it with a masked pleased acceptance, giving the giver the impression that it's what you always wanted.

The radio operator informs us of basic details. A man has been seen standing on the wrong side of the bridge railings across the main dual carriageway spotted by a motorist underneath. He thinks he is a jumper. Chris and I mention the bridge is the same as the one we attended some weeks ago where the man was talked down by local police officers. Was this the same person? Was this an attention seeker, or someone who was desperately depressed and feeling they had no other option but to summon the nerves to step that one more step into utter freedom and an end to every single worry and pain they have.

It only takes 4 minutes to arrive on the bridge. There is a parked car next to the railing with its hazards flashing. I believe it's his. Chris has hardly stopped the car before I'm dragging myself out of it towards the figure standing in the darkness exactly as described by the passer-by. He's on the wrong side of the railings. The young man, in his 20s tall and slim with several days beard growth is swinging like a drunken sloth with one hand on the railing at waist height, rolling his foot to the other side of his other leg and swinging back again. He has a bottle of beer in his other hand. This is different, I don't like this. This is serious. Not that I don't take the others seriously but sometimes with the all too familiar "cry for help" the soul is crying out for a rope to grab hold of, and you simply have to find the words to create that rope, and with some encouraging words gently pass it towards them where most will happily grab hold of it with both hands to be hauled back over to safety. The human mind feels regenerated to do battle with the demons once more.

But I felt that adrenaline in my stomach. This was different. He wasn't supposed to be swinging his body around like a drunk walking down the high street where he would most likely crash into some bins and spill into the road. There were no bins here and the only way to fall was to his death, and it was clear he simply didn't care. He shouts at me, screams at me to stay back. I freeze to the spot and put my hand out flat to show I was completely harmless. I am 10 metres away from him, far too far to do anything if he was to show signs he was going to delete this life and maybe be given the chance to press restart.

"Get back, a bit more, a bit more, I can see the light on your foot and if it moves I'm jumping".

I knew I was stuck to the spot. One little move and he screamed and made me go back another foot from where I was before. This was terrible. The traffic had been stopped below and was building up on either side. I knew this was going to cause chaos but that bit wasn't important. I hated being here now; I needed to get him over that bar. I talked, and he talked, and he shouted and screamed in frustration at a system he felt had let him down.

"They don't help me, you said last time they would help me but I get kicked out, I need help, I can't go on".

He tilts his head right back to collect the final remnants of the beer from his bottle, his eyes pointing skywards when he stumbles. I gasp and step forwards as he loses grip of the bottle to settle himself with his other arm on the barrier, the bottle reminding us both of the height with several seconds silence before a smash of glass below. Far from shocking him, the look in his eyes is of disappointment that there was a chance lost. Keep positive, everything positive I tell myself. I repeat to him, "You will feel better, Shaun, you will look back on this time and be so grateful you didn't jump, you feel terrible now but I promise you, there will be a time soon where you will feel so much better"

I am shivering from the cold and I feel my jacket put over my shoulders. I'm so grateful to Chris, who guessed my need, and I can hear him reporting back the progress or lack of, to the radio operator. I can hear there are units on the front of the road block in both directions, and fire and paramedics are in place on standby. The radio operator says in my ear he has a 4 year old child and he has previously said how he wants to be a good role model for him. I use that, "Shaun, I know you have a little 4 year old who loves his Daddy, yes?"

"Yes", he replies, "But I am a failure to him, little Sam, he's with his Mum and I can't be with him. I can't get help for the things in my head".

It is risky calculating whether to use something that is so emotional to Shaun or not. My words could have been the memory that triggers him to jump, but I press on, "You know that Sam will grow up and will never get over the fact his Daddy committed suicide. You need to be there for him, even if it is when he is much older, but you can't do this to your little boy now".

He quietens, and then he leans towards the car door next to the railing and opens it. "I can help you with that, what do you need?"

"Get back now", he hisses at me, "And further, I know you are trying to grab me, well I will jump unless you get back further".

I shuffle back and I then proceed to watch him put his hand into the door pocket and grab some tobacco. Whilst doing this, I talk calmly and quietly to him. His body is relaxed and I am surprised to see him throw one leg over to the road-side of the railing, but my hopes dashed again when it was simply to get a better reach for more tobacco, before he is back over to his original precarious position.

Half an hour more and I feel there is some progress, it's getting a little lighter now, just slightly and there is some definition to what was once just a silhouette of the trees. We eventually reach an agreement he will come with me once he has had his last cigarette. He says he trusts me. I have given him everything to show I am not going to play hero by making a grab for him or to then bundle him into the nearest police van. I know I have to live up to my promise or he won't trust me again if we find ourselves in a similar position.

And then the most surreal thing happened, I was getting to know Shaun. I got to know some of his demons circling around his head and with some of the feelings he was telling me. I struggled to find a positive in life to introduce to him. Just hope and listening was all I could offer. He'd been promised enough false promises in life before, and they stopped working a long time ago. He talked a lot but then he suddenly went very quiet and he turned away from the bridge letting go with both hands just standing on the thin ledge not a foot wide. He fell silent and bent both his knees as if a small child summoning the courage to jump off a chair.

"Shaun!"

"Shaun!"

Nothing, no reply, nothing, but the casual drop of his spent cigarette end into the darkness, one more adjustment with his feet, and then he followed. There were a few seconds of silence, and then a sound I will never forget.

30. Taser - A Tool For The Pacifists

I wrote this blog to highlight how much my experiences had shown Taser was saving lives, and I wanted to counter the negative views spouted by those who knew nothing about them, but merely thought it was a tool for police to torture innocent members of the public. This was a true account of an incident I was involved in and not adjusted in any way for dramatic value!

I've got a G36 rifle strapped to my chest and a Glock 9mm pistol on my hip. I'm dressed in blacks and have a balaclava over my face. I probably look a bit forbidding to be honest, but so do the other 3 officers to my right stooped below the line of the window. They have a "red key" door enforcer ready and waiting and a first aid kit rucksack splayed open in readiness for things if they take a turn for the worse. He's getting more drunk and volatile and we need to end this safely as soon as possible. I gaze around the room through the window and notice the table on its side with hack marks across the polished surface, and the slashes in the plasterboard wall. The woman is shaking. She's his mother and a domestic has occurred. He's flipped and is now holding her hostage threatening to kill her. We have been called by a neighbour and we have managed to pull some sort of a plan together. Something for us to take minutes to organise, and for the lawyers to take months to pull apart.

Contingencies are set. Some fatal ones in case he decides to run at his mother on seeing us. We will be criticised if we end up shooting him. Why didn't you wait it out and let him sober up? Okay, so we shall wait, but then he gets more drunk and emotional and the result is the same. We will be criticised. I gave up a long time ago caring what impossible critics thought. There is only one person I have to satisfy we did the right thing, and that is the one standing in my shoes looking at this scene.

I call out in a calm but firm manner to the male. The guys are ready to go, poised. The male fronts up, puffs his chest out and screams at me, I fire... a Taser. 'Clackackackackack', he stiffens and reaches taller than he's ever been before, and then with a sigh like a deflating cushion, he folds over onto the carpet in front of the settee. "GO GO GO" I shout and the guys are off, the door forcer crashing through the conservatory doors swinging in on themselves with glass shattering for metres around, the wooden frame twisting and snapping as several size 10 boots crash over it.

The Taser cycle of 5 seconds ends and the male is jumping up enraged, pulling off his T-shirt and therefore the barbs in his chest. The contact is broken, I see progress is slower than I had hoped and there is a moment of concern, before the dead cartridge drops to the floor and I swing its replacement on the front and fire again, both barbs making contact with his bare chest and down he goes again. My colleagues are forcing their way in past a barricade and on to his rigid body. It's 30 seconds and he's in handcuffs, his mother is led away in tears and the shattered house is boarded up to protect it from the elements. This wasn't Manchester. This was Willand near Cullompton in Devon. One neighbour reported a disturbance, the others had no idea what had gone on, there were no waiting press, no one went to hospital, and myself and my officers wrote a statement and then attended a road collision after that. Life carried on, but a Taser saved a life that night, and nobody knew, or cared.

Taser is a brand name, but if I called it a conducted electrical weapon, you may not read further. I am not going into the technical bits which are quite complicated and involve inventors of mystical powers, but I can speak from experience and tell you what I saw. I have seen it save life. I have seen incidents prevented from developing just by the red dot being switched on, and I have seen it have little and no effect also.

Here's the deal. I have one, I am fortunate to have one, as I can hide behind it when a little bit scared! Other officers don't get that opportunity. You see the phrase once bitten twice shy comes into being and so usually the sight of it or knowledge an officer has it can subdue a subject without the need to deploy it fully. Once Tasered they find it really hurts and you won't want to repeat the experience. So are police going around torturing poor old members of public? Are poor individuals dying from being Tasered left right and centre, and as a councillor said to me recently, until people stop dying, we should keep to traditional means. I despair at this ignorant view; mainly as the violent aggressor who wants to rip the throat from the officer gets to not be Tasered but the officer has to suffer the huge and horrific injuries for the pleasure.

I am glad to listen to advice and opinions, but from experience or knowledge, not from people who have tv programmes and media chat to go by. Let's get rid of some myths shall we?

1. Taser will stun you and knock you out - no it won't. It will affect your muscles in a way a bit like cramp. I mean horrendous cramp, and the person will fall over and rarely be injured. I said that and I mean it. As long as you don't Taser someone on the edge of a cliff or tall building, they are usually completely unharmed.

2. The Taser always works and so can be relied upon - no it won't. We all saw the video in the London Tube station when several attempts were made without success. The Taser fires two barbs. They have to be far enough apart to get a good spread. If the suspect has thick clothing, it may not work. Hit them with one barb, it won't work. Try hitting a person with both barbs as they are trying to stab you with a knife and running towards you at speed. Given this situation, I would not risk my life by hoping my barbs both hit and have the desired effect. I would have to use a Glock 9mm pistol as my very last resort. I would of course hope to Taser them earlier if given the opportunity or use a Baton gun (AEP) to stop it developing into this situation from a safer distance but there are too many variables with a Taser not working and with its restricted distance ability. I won't bet my life on me hitting a charging knife man with my Taser. It would be the

271

Glock. Rather be judged by 12 than carried by 6.

3. Tasers kill lots of people. No they don't. If someone has a heart condition and under extremely rare circumstances dies because of being Tasered, then at least I am alive. I don't think that is harsh. It was me or them. Taser will not be used on an annoying person. There is strict training and legislation such as the Human Rights Act. Don't believe all the rubbish you hear on social media. Police officers do not go round wishing to torture the public.

4. There aren't enough checks on the Taser to establish facts. - wrong. It fires confetti with thousands of the same serial number on so each fired cartridge is traceable to the user. The Taser measures the specific time it fired, the date, the temperature of the air at the time, it measures the length of time the trigger was pulled on the subject and it measures how many times the trigger was pulled and for how long.

5. Police will use it all the time, Truncheons and Batons break arms and legs. They cause bones to break. Having been Tasered and then easily controlled by the officer, with no struggle or after effect, the person is 100% fit to stand up and behave in a normal way, straightaway, when the trigger is released. No recovery time is required. Say that to an offender with a broken arm.

I have seen the Taser used on someone self-harming. Sound a bit tough? Well it's the perfect tool to use when you realise negotiation is failing to save a person's life. There is some poor soul so desperate with the serrated edge of a kitchen knife against her wrist in the bedroom flat, tears running down her face, drug-induced psychosis, and not willing to listen to calming reason. She glares her eyes at me, and strains her face, and begins to scream long and loud like an injured animal. I know I have lost the situation as she slowly but firmly saws the knife across into her wrist. I hear a "Clat" then "clatatatatatat" and the girl falls like a tree slowly being felled, across the bed and onto the floor. My colleague has fired his Taser next to me. Whilst the Taser is still on, I can calmly walk over to her, bend down and gently pick the knife up between my finger and thumb with no danger to myself. I then walk away. The woman is unharmed, the police officers are unharmed and the knife is recovered. The woman is now able to receive some mental health assistance.

As an Armed Response Sergeant, I carry a Baton, pepper spray, Taser, Glock and I have other larger weapons available within seconds. The order of force we use is this. After having tried negotiation and officer presence, Taser would be first choice, then pepper spray if no Taser available, then Baton in that order for a very good reason. Taser has no recovery period. The subject is 100% well immediately. Pepper spray is just horrible and you will create so much snot and mucus for nearly an hour afterwards it really isn't a pleasant substance. Try rubbing a chilli in your eyes and you will get an idea, as that is the main component of pepper spray, a synthetic chilli for an accurate consistent deployment. Then there is the traditional Baton. I don't know about you, but although the pain is horrible for the Taser at least as an offender I won't be in hospital from a Baton strike.

Generally people understand that police are good people who want to help others. But there are others who feel Police will want to torture people if given the tools to do so, which is what the main critics fear. Trust us to do the job, or change the police force you have. Officers are getting injured by horrible means whilst this decision is batted about.

I have also found that as an Armed Response officer, having attended the address earlier with the male holding his mother hostage, when we were called to the address again some weeks later, a by product was that he could not have been more polite. They don't like it you know. The public are able to claw back some control from the streets.

Tasers are expensive, very expensive, about £750 each and about £20 for each cartridge. Fine until you realise they have a use-by date and as well as the training of each officer, you have to pay for the refresher training. There is a cost. But take it from me, who has been at the bottom of a violent mob trying to do me great damage as recently as last year, when I thought I was really in trouble and knew they could get away with anything at that point, I decided not to use the Taser on them. I knew they would get it off me and use it against me as there were so many more of them than me. So it's not the solution to everything. It is a tool, one tool, and if ever replaced for armed cover, may your error never come back to haunt you, as when you need it to work the most, it may not.

Control rooms sending Taser officers to violent persons with knives thinking they are covered with Taser will be bitten one day. We will attend a Police funeral before long if some continue to do that. By all means get the Taser there to protect the public in the interim, but get the Armed Response there too so they can use other less lethal options at greater distances and have a conventional solution if all other efforts have been considered, tried, but failed.

Tell me it doesn't work, when I walked into a pub with my firearms colleagues to deal with a man after a domestic standing at the bar with a machete stuffed in his waistband and him carrying invisible carpets under each arm with raised veins like he'd just done 10 bench presses. Tell me that him throwing the machete to the floor and putting his hands on his head wasn't the best solution just because the red dot appeared on his chest. No trigger pulled, not even any pain, but tell me that Taser shouldn't be used because the occasional person has a heart attack after trying to kill a police officer because they have a heart condition. My sympathy is rather lacking on that one. If you are a pacifist then I suggest you hope that every police officer has access to a Taser. And trust in their training, their judgement, and by all means sack the ones that have alternative motives. You will be shocked by how few of those there are.

31. The Knot is Getting Tighter

I wrote this blog about my colleague Tanja who I asked permission to write a blog about an incident she feels probably ended her career due to PTSD. Very little has been changed because I wanted to emphasise how important it was to support officers who don't have the social support they used to have some years ago.

20 years ago, we played cards over breakfast with the Section in the Station Canteen. We had already decided who would rush out to the next job if disturbed. We played rugby together, we finished a late shift at 10pm and quickly went to the already bustling bar in the station for a beer before time was called before we walked home. We had a Christmas pantomime where we took the mick out of ourselves, especially the bosses. We went to the police ball and enjoyed leaving dos attended by many, because we all lived nearby. We defused.

Now we all live 20 miles from work. Response officers once briefed will work single-crewed and attend many jobs just as Tanja did. They will attend cot deaths, fatal car crashes, sudden deaths, be assaulted and have many complaints made against them by unscrupulous people who have an axe to grind. They have no canteens, no bars, and put up with some journalists who complain when they see them buy food or have a cup of tea in public with their colleagues. A leaving do consists of a drink in a nearby bar with 5 or 6 colleagues as no one stays in the same department for long now. There are no pantomimes as the facilities have gone and there are no police balls because the community has gone. Those single-crewed officers often drive home to their empty houses and deal with the same additional private life problems we all have to deal with, but on top.

This isn't healthy. We have TRIM (Counselling) and Wellness campaigns designed to improve our mental health. It is being recognised by the police service, but it may well be too little too late after any traumatic event. We need to bring the community feeling back into policing but I fear it's probably too late and I worry for the mental health of officers in the future. I wrote this blog to highlight a particular case one of my response officers attended. Tanja gave me permission to use her name.

Tanja swings the Astra patrol car into the driveway. "Ah great", she remarks, "The family are here. We can get on with this". She's careful how she opens the driver's door. She doesn't want the family to see her hit their car parked next to her. That would not get them off on the right footing. Tanja's crew mate Jo jumps out of his seat and is already on his way over to a woman in her mid 40s who's standing on the front door step. Her 18 year old daughter is looking bored next to her. It's 9.30 on a cold Boxing night, and the first thing Tanja notices is the nervousness on the mother's face.

The house is a Victorian semi-detached. It's substantially built with wooden framed windows. It's been well looked after and the family look quite well-to-do.

"I'm getting a little worried now", the woman says as Tanja catches Jo up near the front door. Jo asks the usual questions regarding the woman's concern and why the police response unit have been called. Her 15 year old son had refused to go out with his Mum and sister to visit friends that evening, so they had left him at home. He had been acting a little strangely but she had put it down to being a teenager. It's just one of those teenage times they have to get through. But the concern had begun to grow since they had tried to phone him several times that evening on both his mobile and on the house phone. She had received no answer from him. They decided to come home early but now they couldn't get into their own house. They were at a loss as to what to do next.

Jo disappears around to the side of the house. It's cold enough to leave a trail of breath in his wake which dissipates through the light thrown from the street light. Tanja knocks loudly on the front door, pushing the doorbell repeatedly. "Simon!" she shouts through the letterbox. "It's the police here now. We will have to break our way in if you don't answer the door". She turns the key the woman has left in the lock, but it has no effect. The dead lock is on. Tanja glances at the woman and daughter and comforts them. "Don't worry, this happens all the time. It's probably an attention thing, these teenagers, hey?"

The woman forces a half smile and anxiously turns towards the direction where Jo had disappeared. He comes around panting slightly, "I've had a look, and there's no obvious way in. He's not answering my knocking."

"Okay, we'll make it as minimal damage as we can", Tanja says to the woman, "Are you happy for us to continue?"

"Yes, there's nothing else we can do is there?".

Tanja gets her Baton out of her police utility vest and without hesitation, taps the corner of a pane of glass twice. The glass smashes immediately and large pieces fall inside. This is enough to allow her to get her arm through to turn the lock from the inside. Jo turns the door key at the same time and the door swings open.

The house is in darkness except for the light from the street light opposite. There's no noise, quite eerie really. Tanja pushes past Jo. She's keen to show she's a little annoyed now and even more so when she gazes through the hallway and there standing as upright as a statue is the figure of a young man. "Simon!" Tanja shouts in annoyance, "You have totally wasted our time and your Mum's". Tanja fumbles for a light switch getting ready to give her wrath to the 15 year old, the lights flicker on and Tanja spins her head round to face Simon again.

She stares at him, taking in the scene for a second but holding her breath, she looks at his eyes staring at her but something stops her going further. She gazes at him up and down and then feels an icy shudder flow over her body as if she were wearing nothing but a nighty in this -3 degree temperature.

Her face moves from anger to confusion to fear, "OUT, OUT, GET THEM OUT JO!" She swings around grabbing at the front door and pushes him out towards the two women. He's already realised and doesn't need any persuasion, and is spinning the mother around on her heels, pushing her down the front step towards the patch of frosty grass. The door slams closed behind him leaving Tanja inside staring at the broken glass left on the floor. She dreads looking at him again, but there's a creaking sound that forces her to, a creak that only comes from a thick rope twisting with a heavy weight on the end.

She stares at the 4 inch space between his toes and the floor. She slowly gazes up from his bare feet to his jeans then on to his pale hands hanging loosely beside him; then on to his faded Harry Potter T-shirt. A well-built young man, athletic, and she continues to look up to the rope around his neck, his round young pale face with a horrible contorted expression. Her eyes followed the half-inch thick rope up from his neck to where it was very well fastened to the top banister rail. This rope was not going to snap.

Tanja was already holding his legs realising she had shut Jo out. The sounds of confusion outside meant mother and daughter had not seen the terrible scene of her beloved son hanging there for her to see when she'd got home. But Simon was obviously dead. There was no recovering him. Jo came back in again and between him and Tanja, managed to cut the body down. The ambulance was on scene very shortly afterwards, but no attempt was made by them once they'd realised he'd been dead some time.

Tanja had 4 days off after that night. Just rest days by a stroke of luck, but it turned out to be very bad luck. She wasn't able to talk the job through with her colleagues, and when she did go back to work, she threw herself into it with gusto, to shake those haunting thoughts of poor Simon hanging there from her mind. And it was only when she was tackling a drunk with her colleagues a couple of nights later, when she was struggling to get the handcuffs on him, that she realised something was wrong. Something was very wrong; she didn't feel herself, and she was scared because she didn't know why.

Tanja has now left the police. She suffers from PTSD but has got on with her life and is doing very well having received counselling. This account is very much based on real events she witnessed and suffered.

32. Car Collision

This blog is about a true account that I was involved in, in the last few years. I wanted to explain how hard it is on the witnesses as well as the officers and other emergency services, let alone the family. I wanted to show how it was all so avoidable and how much work goes into these cases. They happen all too often however. I thought it important to try to make the reader feel they were there at the time.

It was warm which was always a bonus, one less thing to worry about at 3 o'clock on this dark and very still morning. The single car involved was completely unrecognisable. It was dry and only a slight breeze caressed the branches of the trees around my head. I had travelled at speed for over an hour to get here. I knew it was too late to save life, but any delay meant even longer to open the road, but more importantly, I needed to get there to ensure no vital evidence or witnesses were lost. I had learned over the years there was a thin line between patronising skilled and experienced officers and ensuring they had done things correctly.

When I joined the police back in 1990 as a 21 year old, I have to say I was well out of my depth and I always felt I was the one who managed to fool the interview board into giving me a punt. It had taken 2 goes at the 3-day assessment, and on the second attempt, I almost didn't get in because my blood pressure was so high. But here I was, standing at the scene of a double fatal road traffic collision, and in charge of the investigation.

I had ensured all witnesses were accounted for, and the next of kin of the crash victims were being tracked down by family liaison officers. I'd managed to get a witness account from another car driver who had seen this car careering towards him. "I KNEW I WAS IN TROUBLE OFFICER", he stammered. Not because he had done anything wrong, but because a huge angry metal monster had been charging down on him, spitting fire and metal shards, smashing through trees, a spinning whirlwind with debris shooting in all directions like fireworks. The car took one hesitant pause as it balanced precariously on its rear end, before slowly tumbling over like a felled tree onto what was left of its wheels. The witness had seen all this happen in front of him. And as the car settled, he stared at it. It breathed steam from its mouth, it breathed its last and then, silence.

It was dark, very dark in this country road, a main route between two large towns, but it was quiet for now. The witness had gingerly got out of his car, and hesitantly made his way towards the mangled wreckage. He used the lights of his car to light the wreckage, but he found he was causing a shadow across the scene blocking his view from his headlights, so he slowly approached it from the verge with his phone torch switched on. He hesitantly gazed into the car, every panel smashed to pieces or crushed to an unrecognisable form. His eyes followed the light into the depths of the car and he saw the twisted bodies inside, two of them, a youngish male and female. There was no obvious car door to open, it was as if it were welded to the crushed bodywork of the car, no hinges would help him here. He listened then whispered through the dimly lit gloom.

"Hello?"

He pressed number 9, three times on his phone realising his finger was shaking uncontrollably. He was surprised at the lively reply on the phone, "Which Service please?"

His voice shaking, "AMBULANCE, FIRE... POLICE, JUST GET EVERYONE HERE".

He crumpled as one of the ghostly faces entered his mind. His first flashback, it was just the three of them in that space and he burst into tears. The first police officers arrived soon after although it seemed an age. He calmed the man with soft tones. It's often difficult to establish what could have gone on to cause such a collision at this early stage. The fire service did an amazing job by freeing one of the bodies, but then held off as I needed to keep the car intact for the vehicle examiner to examine the car. The male remained contorted inside. It's no good cutting the car to pieces to free the bodies only to find the car falls apart on lifting it onto the back of a recovery truck. That would potentially destroy the steering rack, the brake lines and any potentially vital clues that would tell us the cause of the loss of control. It will inevitably be too much speed but we can't ever take that for granted. So the last body stays in the car for the next few hours until the scene examination is done. An officer has already ensured some dignity for the occupants by covering them as much as he can with blankets. It's some time before I can give the go ahead for the Fire Service to come back and cut the final one out. It seems harsh, but it's important. The cause for this was going too fast for the circumstances, and simply losing control, getting caught up in the moment, which left two families utterly devastated for the rest of their lives.

33. We Need You but We Don't Want You

I wrote this blog in reaction to the very strong possibility of officers having to be segregated for hours from their colleagues after a police shooting had occurred. I have taken a number of incidents I have been involved in to write this piece in order to outline the concerns I had. I have spoken to many colleagues who have been involved in shootings to get a better feeling of how being treated post-shooting can be. It was having read this blog, the Deputy Commissioner of the Independent Police Complaints Commission, (IPCC) at the time, Sarah Green came down from London to Devon to speak to me for a couple of hours on the subject. The idea of segregation soon lost steam. I doubt this blog had a direct impact but it's nice to think it added to the general resistance in some way and has ultimately protected other officers from inhumane treatment.

"Where, Si, where is he?" I repeated as I screamed the car into the dark car park. A man who'd been sent to prison for 10 years for a horrific assault with a knife on his wife was out again, and he had smashed a glass fish tank over her head this time. She was in a bad way and he was on the run with a 12" kitchen knife. He's been seen by CCTV entering the car park but it's dark, very dark, and my headlights are scanning across the car park. Adrenaline surges through my veins as Si and I prepare ourselves. I mumble under my breath and Si turns his head towards me. "He's going to fight, mate", I said, "He has a lot to get away for."

My partner was Simon that night, and we had just been authorised for a firearms incident. The man had a knife on him. He had used one 10 years previously on the same woman, so we knew he was capable of using it. Okay we had Glock 17's in holsters but against knives it's often very useful to have the AEP (Baton gun) available from the car safe. This is a less lethal option which means we can try to knock an armed suspect off their feet from a distance. That would not only prevent the man from getting away to do more harm, it would also stop him being shot if he's still wielding the knife in front of us.

"There!" Si shouts urgently from the passenger's side, "There, Harry, there!" I'm searching through the gloom and can see, through the darkness quite a distance ahead, a trainer catching the glow from the street light. I speed towards the man. Si updates the Comms room and we close in. I throw the BMW past the suspect who is sprinting for an alleyway. My only option is to get ahead and cut him off.

I pull up sharply ahead, and shout, "You ready, Si?" It's not an ideal scenario – the suspect is now physically close – but if he makes it to the alleyway we could lose him, and that would be a disaster. If he runs for Simon with the knife there will be no time to be sure that a Taser will hit both barbs at a good spread through thin enough clothing. No time either to level aim and shoot a baton gun. Only enough time for a reflex shot with the H&K G36 carbine rifle strapped across Simon's chest. Batons and Tasers fail too often. It's not a precise science and I won't risk my life or my colleague's hoping they will be effective when someone is rushing me with a knife.

Si, jumps out and challenges, "ARMED POLICE, STAND STILL". The suspect darts to the side and Si gives chase. Si doesn't see the knife and so he doesn't shoot. I jump out of the car and sprint after him towards the alley. We are wearing a lot of heavy gear and this race has to end soon or we will lose it. From running at full speed the man suddenly slows, throwing his hands up in surrender, "Okay, Okay".

He was arrested, we found the kitchen knife in his belt, and he went back to prison for a long time. The woman lived, but barely. And after we had booked this chap in we went back to work; a road traffic collision and a noisy group of youths, I believe.

Now having dealt with numerous incidents just like this, and having levelled the red dot sights of my rifle at a man carrying a gun who had just carjacked a car salesman, I know all too well how these incidents could so easily have turned out differently. So far I have been very fortunate. The man with the gun stared at me... Was it death by cop? Was he going to level it at me in the hope I end things for him? Or was he going to try to get a reputation in prison for shooting a police officer? As my red dot in my sights danced around his chest, echoing the rise and fall of my deep breathing, and the police helicopter above relayed everything back to the comms room, I knew I couldn't let my colleague down. I must follow the simple rules. Simple but deadly. If he raises that gun at me or my colleague, then I shoot...

He dropped the gun, and went back to prison for 10 years.

But over my 20 or so years on front-line Armed Response policing, in which I have been an operational firearms commander, a tactics advisor, and completed a Post Incident Management course, I have known of several shootings and known the officers involved very well. None of them had an easy ride post-incident and it still continues today. They were all pretty much dragged through the mill. The result is that the IPCC are not trusted by armed police officers. It is felt by most there is a hunger to feed when a police shooting occurs. A hunger to ensure the families of the deceased feel satisfied with the investigation, no matter how unreasonable their demands are. Politics enters. Threats of riots are common.

I don't feel safe anymore. I will do as I always have done. I only have to satisfy myself, knowing I had no alternative and that my actions were proportionate, reasonable and necessary. But these judgements are not a precise science and if you play by the sword as a criminal, you may just die by the sword one day. However hard I have tried to do my job to the very best of my ability the moment after a shooting is going to be filled with trauma. The IPCC are suggesting that officers be separated after a shooting until after they have given their accounts. This may sound reasonable but I want you to imagine what it's like after a shooting.

The gun goes off. There is a momentary silence as both officers can't quite believe what has happened. The

289

officers glance at each other and the man falls to the ground. He's not motionless like on a cop film. He's kicking and thrashing about. The officers sprint up to him with their advanced medic pack, ripping it open. One has the scissors, cutting up the sleeves and body of the shirt to reveal the man's chest. One tries to push celox gauze - a clotting agent in a bandage - into the wound which is pumping blood. They struggle with him to stop him moving so they can treat him, but he's fighting. He soon becomes weak. Another officer opens the defibrillator pack. The male is motionless now, his eyes fixed. The officers are slipping on fluid. They think it is rain from the road but it is blood. They are pumping on the man's chest, defib pads applied, and the machine is speaking demands in clear slow robotic tones... "Stand clear of patient" The officers lean back on their haunches... their faces are drained, their eyes wide and black and they are covered in blood as they stare at each other.

They are in a room at the police station 15 miles away. The procedures are in place and the IPCC has been called. Local investigation teams are controlling the scene and containing any evidence. The officer's weapon that was fired is left in situ. There are two principal officers and from staring at each other back on that street, they are now separated, alone in a room in the police station, sitting with only a faceless chaperon. They are in a daze. The world swirls around their heads.

One is looked at by the medic. One sits and waits in another room. His chaperon doesn't know what to say or indeed what he can say. He offers a drink of coffee.

A minute feels like an hour. Nothing. Something smells. He glances down and sees the heavy congealed blood on his vest. The spare magazine still in its pouch, the silver bullets smeared with blood. He checks himself over quickly. He is covered, even his hair; he must have put his hands through it. He feels dirty. He feels disgusting. He wants to shower and get this stuff off his face. He thinks of his wife and his little girl. How did it come to this? Hours go by. He cannot talk. The IPCC have to travel some distance. They can delegate urgent work but the waits are always hours and hours. The officers sits on in silence. He looks at his smartphone, stupidly views what is on it. "Police shoot unarmed grandad of two". A doting picture of his victim stares up at him with two children on his lap. "What have I done? Those poor kids, Christ, I'm going to jail, how did this all happen?"

An investigator comes into the room with a piece of paper. "We need you to write down exactly what happened". They leave.

It will be months before the truth comes out. Months to show how the grandad of two attempted to kill him with a machete whilst under a drug-induced psychotic episode. It's old news by then and very little of this detail makes it into the media. Months of teasing for his daughter in the school playground, months of wondering if he's going to jail, immense pressure on his marriage, months of hearing the subjects family being apologised to and months of self-doubt.

Armed Response Officers are volunteers. Quite for how much longer, I don't know.

34. Spit Hoods/Guards. To Use or Not to Use?

I wrote this blog to highlight how necessary it was for officers to have spit hoods available to them, even though they may only be used on very rare occasions. This is a true account and I wanted to have the reader feel the same as myself and my colleagues. It was to fight the ridiculous argument the spit hoods degraded the wearer with no care at all to the mental and physical wellbeing of the officer. Again, this is a very true account of what happened to me, and one I won't forget in a hurry.

I'm single-crewed coming off the motorway at the end of a late shift. The radio operator says, "You are wanted on channel 181".

I flick across channels sitting at the main junction 30 of the M5 motorway and introduce myself to the new operator. "You are wanted at Exeter Custody. They have a situation there where they may need a Taser"

I have a Glock 9mm and a G36 semi-automatic and a Baton gun, all safely secured, but I also have Taser and pepper spray. A little array of delights, each suited for a particular incident which may arise, constantly assessed and re-assessed to ensure I choose the correct option in a split second of decision-making. I blue-light it to custody and press the intercom button. The door immediately opens which highlights their haste. Scanning the monitors the custody Sergeant points to one which has a pink glow to it. "Strange, didn't know you had a chill out-room?" I say.

"We don't" he replied, "That's blood. He's poured water all over his cell floor and cut his wrists".

I know the detained person who's very violent and suffering from an extreme mental health issue. This man had been holding a street to ransom climbing onto roofs and throwing slate tiles like frisbees for 100's of metres around. He is now lying completely naked in a foetal position against the wall with his back to the centre of the room.

"Slashed his wrists?" I ask. It is clear I am wondering who messed up with this one.

"He managed to smash his toilet and used the sharp edge of the bowl. That's where all the water has come from. We are calling some public order officers in but it's taking time."

My other Armed Response unit is now with me. We all go down to the cell with a detention officer. "It's hard to tell how bad his cut is with that water and blood, and he's been still for too long for my liking. Guess there's no time to wait!"

I nod to the detention officer and he cracks the door open. I move in immediately finding the floor extremely slippery. My Taser packed safely away because of the water. I call out to him, but there's no movement, and no answer. I move closer and see his pale body looking drained of blood. I hasten my step and touch his torso to feel the temperature. His head facing the wall still and still no response. I tug at his side and I feel a smack of something in my face and mouth, no time to react but step back and fall over, he's spun around and is fighting. I am grabbing at him to get a grip of him somehow but he's like a wet fish at the bottom of the boat writhing about and he is too slippery, my only hope is to work him towards the door where my colleagues can help me control him. Now we have him outside in the dry corridor, we are constantly fearful of positional asphyxia where we know we will be up for manslaughter, so no weight on his chest or his back, but it is still impossible to control his slippery torso especially when you are thinking not only for the moment but for the inquest further down the road. He had huge strength and was tossing us about like rag dolls, and I was beginning to think we had lost this one.

"Taser, Taser, Taser" I hear, and we jump back. Simon fires the Taser and our fighter is now arched and motionless. I view where the barbs are and realise I can get a cuff on, then the other is safely applied, and now all four of us are panting huge gasps of air.

I can taste the metallic taste of blood in my mouth. My mind goes back to my first encounter with him in the cell and realise he has hit me with a well-aimed lump of phlegm. I spit on the ground but I know it's too late. I feel disgusted, especially as I know this man has a lifestyle of drugs and poor health. Still that's for another time. We don't have spit hoods so we have to just ensure his head is turned the other way. An ambulance arrives; his wrists are not too bad. The water has made the blood look more than it actually is. We cover him with a blanket but he's obviously not too shy and kicks it off. Simon gets in to the ambulance with him and later reports that he has been spat at full in the face again. They get to the hospital, and Simon has held the blanket between him and the suspect's face. But as the doctor distracts Simon, he feels another blast of well-aimed phlegm dripping down off his top lip over his mouth. It's ridiculous.

That man is now dead. He died 18 months later from a drug overdose. I wondered for a while whether I was infected with a disease that would affect the rest of my life and the relationship with my wife and children. Simon did the same, until it happened again 3 months later.

It's a no-brainer to me and when people argue that it takes the dignity away from the suspect, then I say more than my dignity was taken that night. I say that we police are feeling like punching bags right now with little judicial, national media or political backup. I fear for the coming generation who have to do it all on much less money and prospects.

I propose, that without Mayoral or other political intervention, spit guards are tried for all Forces as indeed some have them already, especially in Scotland. The Met do not. Not to be placed on every detained person, no cop wants that, but many politicians and public have jumped to the conclusion we do, and that it is some black hood which disorientates the wearer like some Daesh prisoner. Nothing like this at all, they are in fact, a fine mesh which is perfectly breathable and is a hood / guard which is placed over the head to stop any further spitting for those that have previously spat and put on those that threaten or are believed to spit again as in this case.

It's simple, and it's common sense.

35. A Diversion from My Everyday Life

This was my most successful blog. I have taken a couple of incidents and made them one to get what I wanted in the blog to explain certain things I wanted to. I wanted to write a blog that grabbed the reader and dragged them through my experience almost like they were on a roller coaster. It explains the emotions we go through, the panic at the scene initially and the aftermath as well as why there can be such a delay with road closures once the initial scene quietens down. Many online papers published this one and I was flattered with the number of traffic officers from all around the country who showed their support on how accurate it was to the reality. Here goes!

Nothing worse than driving up to a closed road with no explanation, nothing worse than driving past a scene at 4mph after a 2 hour wait to find 6 police officers doing nothing with two on their mobiles. Don't they realise I have missed my appointment and now have to re-arrange it. Don't they realise I have missed my dinner I wanted with my family. Christ, what is this world coming to? Perhaps they could do with some more cuts if they can't be bothered to do simple things like put diversion signs out for people, or get a shifty on so I could have done the things I wanted.

Well strap yourself in, we are going on a bumpy ride.

Serious Road Traffic Collision reported, and I'm on my way. I have done these before, hundreds to be fair, and I know that two of my units are also rushing to the scene. It's about half an hour away on blues and twos but I know a local unit will be there before us. I listen to their update, it's not good and they are trying to get some order of the scene but I can hear the quiver in their voice. This is a fatal. At least one dead.

I immediately organise with my control room for a family liaison officer to attend the scene. It gives them so much credibility with the deceased family if they have done so. The second thing I do is arrange Highways to arrive to set up a diversion. This is whilst driving at speed and ensuring I drive safely for the conditions as I don't want to be the cause of another.

I arrive at the scene and my two other units are arriving with me. The local unit gives me a quick debrief. There are 3 cars at the scene, one on its side in the middle of the road, and another sitting parked with a huge dent in the front of it and the other unceremoniously abandoned in the hedge with devastating damage to it. I need to establish what has happened and quickly.

My units are looking for witnesses, the ambulance is on the scene treating a trapped person in the car on its side, and the fire-fighters are stabilising it so it doesn't topple over and trying to release the casualty as well. The occupant is screaming, it's a good sign until I hear, "I can't feel anything". Her partner is out of the car and has his head in his hands saying, "There was nothing I could do".

He looks scared, very scared. Other motorists caught up in the scene are saying the car on its wheels carried out an overtake where it really shouldn't have and hit the other two vehicles. I send an officer to the driver to carry out a breath test. I will need to do it to all of them, and if too injured, a hospital procedure that will take several hours.

I discover an occupant in the other car in the hedge. She is obviously dead with a terrible head injury, almost decapitated, I cannot tell how old. Her face looks like "The scream" mask with brain matter clearly visible. I see a wedding ring on her finger. I gaze at the key ring with a photograph of a young child swinging from the ignition. A pause, a little reflection, this must be my 150th or so person I have seen like this. At least no children hurt this time. Suddenly the scream of the casualty in the other car spins me around. They are making progress, and the casualty is nearly out. The air ambulance has landed and are making their way over the field with a stretcher.

It's been chaos, but we've gained some order, obtaining witnesses first having secured the driver so we know he won't escape in case he's been drinking or on drugs. When a further witness comes forward and confirms what we suspect about his driving, I make a decision and send my double-crewed unit to arrest the driver for suspicion of causing death by dangerous driving. They leave. I have one double-crewed Armed Response Unit and a local officer. Hopefully, there won't be a firearms incident right now because the local officer will suddenly have a lot on their plate.

The world continues away from this collision and resources are tight, but I manage to secure 2 PCSO's to attend the roadblock to turn traffic back. I have already heard that a motorist has vented off at the local officer for their being no diversion, and the officer gave him short shrift. That will be a complaint later.

I have called for the Collisions Investigation officer (CI) who mark the scene, scan it, and produce highly detailed plans and can give you information about the scene like you wouldn't believe. I need to stop unnecessary boots stamping on my scene, destroying any bulb that can be forensically tested to show whether it was lit or not, the CI can tell me a speed of the vehicles, they can tell me who did what where and when they collided, and whether any car lost control prior to or after the collision.

I call the Scenes of Crime for photos and further forensics, I call the vehicle examiner to the scene as there was a suggestion the brakes could have failed. The procedure to secure and collect the physical evidence takes several hours to plot all 3 cars, the debris, and the road itself. A lot, but if it were your sister, mother or father, would you like us to sweep their body up in the back of the van and have no evidence to prosecute any potential offender, or to never know what happened. It's only an accident after all. Or indeed to show the driver was in fact innocent with defective brakes. Were the brakes cut or eroded? Is it murder, was it indeed an attempt at suicide? We have to find out these things so the Coroner can decide what caused this, and so a criminal court can bring to justice any offender and so importantly, to bring closure to the family.

It's been a while and the scene is quiet. The casualty is gone, the deceased still in the car until the forensics are completed. To remove them will mean cutting the car up and we need to know more first. Fire have already placed a blanket over her to offer some dignity, away from prying eyes. The traffic starts to move, but a lot of it is caught between the roadblock and the scene, and they crawl through. It's been two hours for some. I am on my phone to the Control Room updating them. The Collision Investigator is making his way up from the other side of the Force and will be here soon, and so we can't touch anything now. We have the witnesses' details, all of whom are in shock and will be seen later. We have their initial explanations.

My other ARV is going to the hospital to check on the injured driver, and to try to obtain a breath test. The other one is with the arrested driver beginning a short interview. The drivers of the cars driving by are looking at us and I feel momentarily guilty for not "looking busy" but there is nothing to do right now. The family liaison officer has searched the pockets of the deceased in the car. Not a pleasant job. He has the phone details and is trying to research the address. It has to be correct. He can't get it wrong. But it looks like the officer is texting to passers-by. We are in a group in the middle of the road, and receiving scowls from some motorists driving by...

So I ask you, to use that time in the queue to do one thing. Think about your family. Think how it may be if your loved one was trapped in that car with a severed spine, think if you were never going to see them again. Think that that appointment probably can be

301

rearranged again, and think about the family liaison officer walking towards the house with the children's toys on the garden path. Then when you get back home, hug your family.

The End

Printed in Great Britain
by Amazon